LONGMAN ESL LITERACY

Third Edition

Yvonne Wong Nishio

PEARSON
Longman

Longman ESL Literacy, Third Edition

Pearson Education, 10 Bank Street, White Plains, NY 10606

Staff credits: The people who made up the *Longman ESL Literacy,*
Third Edition team, representing editorial, production, design, and
manufacturing, are: Maretta Callahan, Dave Dickey, Nancy Flaggman,
Irene Frankel, Shelley Gazes, Melissa Leyva, Linda Moser,
Gabriela Moya, and Barbara Sabella.

Text composition: Achebe Diseño, TSI Graphics
Text font: 20/27 Schooltext
Illustrators: Stuart Iwasaki, Paul McCusker, Jill Wood

Library of Congress Cataloging-in-Publication Data

Nishio, Yvonne Wong.
    Longman ESL literacy student book / Yvonne Wong Nishio.— 3rd ed.
        p. cm.
    ISBN 0-13-195102-5 (pbk.)
    1. English language—Textbooks for foreign speakers.
    2. Readers for new literates. I. Title. II. Title: ESL literacy student book.
PE1128.N57 2006
428.2'4—dc22
                                                2005055263

LONGMAN ON THE WEB

Longman.com offers online resources for
teachers and students. Access our Companion
Websites, our online catalog, and our local
offices around the world.

Visit us at **longman.com**.

Printed in the United States of America
ISBN: 0-13-195102-5
1 2 3 4 5 6 7 8 9 10–CRK–11 10 09 08 07 06

Contents

Scope and Sequence

Unit Topics	Vocabulary	Competencies	Literacy Skills
1 **The Alphabet** page 1	• The alphabet • Classroom commands	• Ask and answer questions about names • Follow simple classroom instructions	• Recognize and say the letters of the alphabet • Print capital and small letters • Write first and last names
2 **Numbers** page 22	• Numbers from 1-9 • Addresses • Phone numbers • Classroom commands	• Ask for and give personal information • Ask for and give information about phone numbers and addresses • Initiate and respond to greetings	• Read, say, and write the numbers *0* through *9* • Address an envelope • Fill out a simple form
3 **School** page 41	• Commom classroom objects • Places within a school • Classroom language	• Identify common classroom objects • Identify and ask for the location of important places in a school	• Give information about students' own class and school
4 **Time** page 57	• Numbers from 1-100 • Time • Time of day • Verbs for daily routines	• Tell time • Ask for and give information about time • Inititate and respond to greetings and leave-taking • Identify and name common places in the community	• Read, say, and write numbers *1* through *100*
5 **The Calendar** page 75	• Days of the week, months of the year • *today, yesterday, tomorrow* • Dates	• Give the date for today, yesterday, and tomorrow • Create a calendar for the month • Ask for and give information about date of birth and place of birth	• Recognize, say, and write the days of the week • Recognize and name the months of the year • Recognize abbreviations for days of the week and months of the year • Say and write the date of birth and place of birth

Phonics	Grammar	CORRELATIONS		
		CASAS	**LAUSD**	**LCPs**
	• The verb *be: am, is, are* • Possessive *'s* • Questions with *What*	0.1.2, 0.1.4, 0.1.5, 0.2.1	1a, 2, 11c, IA 1-6, IB 8-12, IIA 15-19, IIB 22, 23, 24, 26, 27	7.06, 8.01
• The sounds *s* (as in *sit*) and *n* (as in *no*)	• The verb *be: is, 's, (you) are* • Questions with *What* and *Do you* • Short answers: *Yes, I do. No, I don't.*	0.1.1, 0.1.2, 0.1.4, 0.1.5, 0.1.6, 0.2.1, 0.2.2, 0.2.4, 6.0.1, 6.0.2	1a, 1bi, 1bii, 2, 3, 4b, 5d, 5f, 5ki, 11a, 11ci, IA 2-7, IB 9-12, 14, IIA 19, IIB 18, 22, 27, 28	7.10, 7.12, 8.02, 8.03, 8.08
• The sounds *p* (as in *paper*), *c* (as in *calendar*), and *w* (as in *work*)	• Questions with *What, Where, When*	0.1.2, 0.1.4, 0.1.5, 0.2.1, 0.2.2	2, 4b, 5d, 5e, 5f, 7b, 8, 11, 13, IA 1-6, IB 8-12, IIA 18-19, IIB 23, 24, 28	
• The sounds *t* (as in *time*) and *g* (as in *get*)	• Simple present: affirmative statements • Questions with *When, What time*	0.1.2, 0.1.6, 0.2.2, 0.2.4, 6.0.1, 6.6.6	1a, 1bi, 1bii, 1c, 2, 4b, 5d, 5e, 5g, 6a, 8b, 11ci, 11cii, IA 1-6, IB 8-12, IIA 19, IIB 23, 24, 28	8.06, 10.04
• The sounds *d* (as in *do*), *y* (as in *you*), and the voiceless *th* (as in *thank*)	• The verb *be: was, were* • Questions with *Do you* and short answers: *Yes I do. No, I don't.* • Questions with *When* and *Where*	0.1.2, 0.1.5, 0.2.1, 0.2.2, 0.2.4, 2.3.2, 6.0.1, 7.2.1, 7.2.3, 7.4.2	1biii, 1biv, 1ci, 1d, 1e, 2, 3, 4b, 5e, 6b, 6c, 7a, 11a, 11ci, 11cii, 13, IA 1-6, IB 8-12, IIA 19-20, IIB 22-28	7.03, 8.05, 9.01, 9.02, 9.03, 9.04, 10.04

CASAS: Comprehensive Adult Student Assessment System
LAUSD: Los Angeles Unified School District (ESL Beginning Literacy content standards)
LCPs: Literacy Completion Points (Florida Pre-Literacy Completion Points Level B. The
following LCPs are covered in every unit: 7.01, 7.04, 7.05, 7.06, 7.10, 7.12, 8.01, 8.08)

Unit Topics	Vocabulary	Competencies	Literacy Skills
6 **Money** page 93	• Coin and bill names • Forms of payment • Forms of identification • *buy, pay, get, get on, take the bus, rent*	• Ask for and give information about the cost of something • Identify common types of transactions with money • Make a purchase using cash, check, or credit card • Make change • Identify and protect important personal information • Politely dismiss telemarketers or other solicitors	• Read, write, and say dollar and cent amounts • Recognize and use U.S. coins and bills • Recognize and add combinations of coins and bills that correspond to a total amount • Read and write checks • Sequence events of a story
7 **The Family** page 114	• Family members • Family relationships • *pick up, dial, talk, hang up*	• Make inquiries and give information about the immediate family • Initiate and respond to introductions • Use the telephone to ask for someone and respond to telephone inquiries	• Name the members of a family • Read, understand, and fill out a form requesting personal information • Sequence events of a story
8 **Food** page 131	• Common foods • Meals • Food preparation • *wash, peel, slice, cook, drink* • *Want, like/don't like*	• Identify common foods and beverages • Express personal likes and dislikes • Order food and beverages at a restaurant • Identify costs of food and beverages • Identify the three basic meals	• Recognize singular and plural forms of nouns • Recognize singular and plural forms of the verb *to be: is/are* • Sequence events of a story
9 **Health** page 147	• Parts of the body • Common ailments and injuries • Emergency situations • Medical personnel	• Make inquiries and give information about health • Identify the components of good health maintenance • Make a doctor's appointment • Give information about health • Call for assistance: police, fire department, and ambulance	• Say and write the parts of the body • Describe and write about feelings • Describe and write common symptoms of illness and injuries • Write a school absence note • Describe and write about an emergency situation • Sequence events of a story
10 **Work** page 165	• Occupations • Workplaces • Work experience	• Identify common occupations • Give information about work experience	• Read and fill out a time card for work • Fill out a job application • Use cursive handwriting to write capital and small letters • Write own signature • Sequence events of a story

Phonics	Grammar	CORRELATIONS		
		CASAS	**LAUSD**	**LCPs**
• The sounds *ch* (as in *check*) and *b* (as in *bus*)	• Questions with *How much, How many, May I, Do you have*	0.1.2, 1.1.6, 1.3.1, 1.3.3, 1.8.2, 6.0.2, 6.0.4, 6.1.1, 7.4.2	2, 5c, 5d, 5g, 11a, 11civ, 12, 15a, IA 1-6, IB 8-12, IIA 18-20, IIB 22-25, 27-28	8.04, 9.05, 10.02
• The sounds voiced *th* (as in *this*) and *h* (as in *he*)	• *This is (my brother).* • Questions with *Who, How many, May I*	0.1.2, 0.1.4, 0.2.1, 0.2.2, 2.1.7, 2.1.8, 7.4.2	1a, 1biii, 1ci, 1d, 2, 3, 4b, 5f, 5g, 5l, 5m, 7, 11a, 11ci, 11cii, 11civ, 13, IA 1-6, IB 8-12, IIA 19-20, IIB 23-28	11.01, 11.02
• The sounds *l* (as in *lunch*) and *sh* (as in *she*)	• Singular and plural forms of nouns • Singular and plural forms of *be: is, are* • Questions with *How much*	0.1.2, 0.2.1, 1.1.7, 1.3.8, 6.0.2, 6.0.3, 6.1.1, 7.2.3, 7.4.2	2, 5c, 11a, 11ci, 11cii, 11civ, 13, 14, 15, IA 1-6, IB 8-12, IIA 19-20, IIB 23-27	12.01
• The sounds *m* (as in *my*) and *f* (as in *fine*)	• *What's the matter? What happened?* • Questions with *How many, Do you, Can you*	0.2.1, 0.2.2, 0.2.3, 2.1.2, 3.1.1, 3.1.2, 3.1.3, 7.4.2	1a, 1bii, 2, 4b, 9b, 11a, 11ci, 13, IA 1-6, IB 8-12, IIA 18-20, IIB 23-28	12.02, 12.03, 14.01
• The sounds *j* (as in *job*) and *r* (as in *restaurant*)	• *Do you want to be . . . ?* • Imperatives	0.1.2, 0.2.1, 4.1.2, 4.1.5, 4.1.8, 4.4.3, 7.1.1, 7.2.3, 7.4.2	1a, 2, 3b, 4b, 4c, 11a, 11ci, 11cii, 11ciii, 13, IA 1-6, IB 8-12, IIA 19-20, IIB 22-29	7.07, 8.07, 10.01

CASAS: Comprehensive Adult Student Assessment System
LAUSD: Los Angeles Unified School District (ESL Beginning Literacy content standards)
LCPs: Literacy Completion Points (Florida Pre-Literacy Completion Points Level B. The following LCPs are covered in every unit: 7.01, 7.04, 7.05, 7.06, 7.10, 7.12, 8.01, 8.08)

About the Author

Yvonne Wong Nishio has served the Los Angeles Unified School District (LAUSD) as a teacher, curriculum coordinator, and adult school counselor over the past 37 years. She has the accumulated experience of teaching all five ESL levels at Evans Community Adult School and was designated a resource/demonstration teacher for the Division of Adult and Career Education (DACE) of LAUSD.

Her pioneering work in ESL literacy includes contributions to the ESL Language Model Standards for Adult Education Programs established by the California Department of Education. Her leadership in the field resulted in the writing of the ESL Beginning Literacy Course Outline for LAUSD.

In addition to writing, Yvonne shares her expertise in the field of ESL literacy by training tutors at public libraries in the Los Angeles area.

Introduction

THE ESL LITERACY STUDENT

Longman ESL Literacy, Third Edition, provides **a basic introduction to English**. The material supports literacy training in English and can be used with students who

- have little or no prior school experience
- have had difficulty with the material and pace of a beginning ESL class
- come from a primary language background that uses a non-Roman alphabet

The Student Book has ten units that are topically organized. Because the content parallels most ESL Level 1 courses, the text can be used alone or as a supplement for those students requiring additional instruction.

Longman ESL Literacy gives beginning level students the opportunity to learn and practice basic skills at a gradual, pedagogically sound pace. The exercises and activities enable students to acquire **communication skills necessary to function in real-life situations**, such as filling out forms, responding to telephone inquiries and taking messages, and calling for assistance and describing emergencies. **Each page is a lesson** that is clear and easy to use. Teachers can immediately see the **communicative purpose** of each activity.

The student outcome projected for the course is that students will have the **fundamental literacy skills** and **basic communicative competence** needed to participate successfully in school, in the workplace, and in the community.

GENERAL TEACHING PRINCIPLES

A unique feature of *Longman ESL Literacy,* Third Edition, is the thorough **integration of the basic language skills**—listening, speaking, reading, and writing. For example, in Unit 3, "School," students begin by reading and listening to new vocabulary (classroom objects). The new

vocabulary is then presented in a conversation model. Students practice the conversation through oral repetition drills and are then asked to write words that match pictures. Students practice the conversation in pairs and incorporate the new vocabulary. After that students practice writing.

Instruction focuses on the development of **receptive skills** (listening and reading) **before productive skills** (speaking and writing). The lessons begin with receptive, low-stress activities. Ample opportunities are provided for students to listen to language and internalize it before they are asked to produce it.

Cooperative learning, including group work and pair practice, is built into each lesson. Activities are designed to move from teacher-directed to **student-centered instruction**. For example, students use new language to learn about their classmates, and then use the new language to talk and write about their classmates and themselves.

The difference in **student learning styles** (visual, aural, and kinesthetic) is often pronounced in a beginning ESL class. *Longman ESL Literacy* offers a variety of activities to match the various learning styles of students. For example, for visual learners there are flashcards, for auditory learners there are listening exercises and oral practice drills, and for kinesthetic learners there are total physical response activities.

NEW FEATURES IN THE THIRD EDITION

Both the *Longman ESL Literacy* Student Book and Teacher's Resource Book were revised, based on suggestions from teachers who have actively used the material, to make the program even more comprehensive and effective. A summary of the new features appears on the following page.

Features of the Student Book

- A **scope and sequence** that highlights vocabulary, phonics, grammar, literacy skills, and competencies.
- **Correlations** to the Los Angeles Unified School District (LAUSD) course outline for ESL Literacy, the Comprehensive Adult Student Assessment System (CASAS), and Literacy Completion Points (LCPs).
- **Procedures for key exercises** that help the teacher with classroom management and the presentation and practice of new language and skills.
- **New illustrations** that portray people of diverse backgrounds and supply clear contexts for the model conversations.
- **Revised content** that offers more practice and addresses the changing needs of students.
- **Stories** for each unit, beginning with Unit 2, that previously were in the Teacher's Resource Book now appear only in the back of the Student Book, allowing students to do extra reading and writing practice at home.
- **Clear cross references** that direct the teacher to the audio CD tracks and to the flashcards in the Teacher's Resource Book, Third Edition.

Features of the Teacher's Resource Book

- An **audio CD**, found in the back of the book, that provides authentic conversation models and numerous opportunities for listening and speaking practice.
- New, easy-to-find **reproducible flashcards** (including the alphabet, numbers, words, pictures, and forms) that provide visual support to enhance students' language acquisition.

- **Revised unit-by-unit teaching notes** that include:
  - competency objectives
  - a preparation list that identifies materials needed for a lesson
  - step-by-step teaching notes
  - tips for classroom management
  - comprehension questions for model conversations
  - expansion activities
  - audioscripts and clear references to the CD track numbers

ACKNOWLEDGMENTS

The author wishes to acknowledge with gratitude the following reviewers for their thoughtful contributions to the development of the third edition of *Longman ESL Literacy:*

Blanca Andrade San Jacinto Adult Learning Center; **Phyllis Barnum** ORT Technical Institute; **Elizabeth Bestul** Santa Clara Adult Education Center; **Linda Blount** Lanier Technical College; **Joan Brandt** Glendale Community College / Adult Community Training Center; **Megan Carroll-Belgarde** Evans Community Adult School (LAUSD); **Hsiuhua Chiang** Chinese-American Planning Council, Inc.; **Ann Marie H. Damrau** San Diego Community College District / Cesar Chavez Campus; **Christopher Davis** Evans Community Adult School (LAUSD); **Susan Gaer** Santa Ana College / School of Continuing Education; **Carol Garcia** College of DuPage; **Ruth Goode** City College of San Francisco; **Mary Jane Jerde** Howard Community College; **Maria Leon** Garfield Community Adult School / Eastside Learning Center; **Xinhua Li** City College of San Francisco / Chinatown; **Teresa C. Luna** Garfield Community Adult School; **Sara Mam** Glendale Community College; **Betty Merriman** College of the Desert; **Doreen Nawatani** Santa Clara Adult Education Center; **Kirk Olgin** Glendale Community College; **Juanita V. Rodriguez** College of the Desert; **Ellen Vanderhoof** Triton College; **Lorena Vega** College of the Desert / EVC; **Andrea Woyt** Triton College

Procedures for Key Exercises

Several key exercises appear regularly in the Student Book. The following pages offer detailed procedures for those exercises, which are identified by their icons and direction lines below. The audio CD and flashcards mentioned in the procedures can be found in the Teacher's Resource Book, Third Edition. Literacy lined paper, also mentioned in the procedures, can be found in the back of both the Student Book and the Teacher's Resource Book.

 Listen to the conversation.

 Practice the conversation.

 Listen and watch the teacher.
Listen again and do.

 Speak and write about . . .

 Write . . .
Listen . . .

 Listen to the story.

 Ask your classmates.

 Talk about your classmates.

🎧 Listen to the conversation.

Reduced Student Book
Page 96, Unit 6

🎧 Listen to the conversation.

🗣 Practice the conversation.

EBC STORE

A: May I help you?
B: How much is this?
A: It's $28.00.
B: I'll take one, please.
A: Cash or charge?
B: Cash.

🪙 Read the words. Write.

| cash | charge | check |

1.

2.

3.

_____ _____ _____

🗣 Practice the conversation with the new words.

96 UNIT 6

Reduced Student Book
Page 96, Unit 6

SET CONTEXT

1. **Books closed.** Show the flashcard or the picture in the Student Book and have students study the picture. **Set the context** of the scene by asking students to say who the people are and where the conversation is taking place.

MODEL

2. **Model** the conversation by playing the audio CD or reading the conversation aloud. **Point** to each speaker as students listen. Have the students listen two or three times.

CHECK

3. To check comprehension, **ask *Yes/No* questions**. Have students answer chorally or individually. Comprehension questions for each conversation can be found in the unit-by-unit notes in the Teacher's Resource Book.

4. If students have trouble answering the questions, **review** the context by having students listen to the conversation again.

PRACTICE

5. Have students **listen and repeat** the conversation. **Point** to each speaker on the flashcard as students repeat the sentence(s).

Practice the conversation.

Listen to the conversation.

Practice the conversation.

A: May I help you?
B: How much is this?
A: It's $28.00.
B: I'll take one, please.
A: Cash or charge?
B: Cash.

Read the words. Write.

| cash | charge | check |

1.

2.

3.

Practice the conversation with the new words.

96   UNIT 6

Reduced Student Book
Page 96, Unit 6

Note: The conversations in Units 1 and 2, as well as some conversations in later units, have blanks. For these conversations, ask students to write their own information in the blanks. Ask various students for their answers and use that information during the drills. Ask students to use their own information when they practice the conversation with their partners and when they write the conversations.

SET CONTEXT

1. **Books closed.** Hold up the corresponding flashcard and review the **context** of the scene by asking students to say who the speakers are and where the conversation is taking place.

DRILL

2. Hold up the flashcard and lead the students in **oral drills**:

Repetition Drills

- Say each line and ask the class to repeat chorally.
- Divide the class into two groups: Speaker A and Speaker B. Say each line and ask each group to repeat their lines chorally.
- Reverse the groups and repeat the conversation.

Question/Answer Drills

- Assign roles. The teacher is Speaker A and asks the question(s) in the conversation. The students are Speaker B and answer the question(s).
- Then reverse roles so that the students are Speaker A and ask the questions.

READ ALOUD 3. **Books open.** Say each line of the conversation and have students **read each line and repeat** chorally. If students have difficulty reading the words, write the conversation on the board or on an overhead transparency. Point to each word as you say the lines aloud. Students read and repeat.

REVIEW 4. Do the repetition drills and the question/answer drills again, but this time with the students reading the conversation.

Note: After students have completed the page, have them **copy** the conversation on literacy lined paper. Literacy lined paper can be found in the back of both the Student Book and the Teacher's Resource Book.

TPR Listen and watch the teacher.
Listen again and do.

> • Take out your check.
> • Write the check.
> • Show your driver's license.
> • Show your credit card.

Write the sentences.

1. _____

2. _____

3. _____

4. _____

Speak and write about how you pay the rent.

106 UNIT 6

Reduced Student Book
Page 106, Unit 6

SET CONTEXT

1. **Books closed.** Describe the **context** and **purpose** of the activity. For example, in Unit 6, tell the students that you are going to write a check. Ask students to give examples of when we write checks (to buy something, to pay a bill, etc.). Review words used in the activity (a check, a watch, a clock, a box, etc.).

DO TPR*

2. Say and perform each command. Ask students to **listen and watch**.

3. Say and perform each command. Ask students to **listen and do** the actions.

4. Say the commands; do not perform them. Ask students to **listen and do** the actions.

5. Say the commands; do not perform them. Ask students to **listen and repeat** at the same time they **do** the actions.

SUBSTITUTE

6. Say the commands and **substitute familiar vocabulary**. For example, in Unit 6, for *Write the check* substitute *Write the time* or *Write the address* or *Write the phone number*. Ask students to demonstrate the actions.

PRACTICE

7. Form pairs or small groups. Ask students to **take turns saying and doing** the original actions. After students have practiced the original commands, encourage them to substitute other vocabulary they know.

---

* Total Physical Response is a language learning approach developed by James Asher. It focuses on language acquisition through non-threatening, physically demonstrated listening comprehension activities.

Speak and write about . . .

Speak and write about . . .

TPR Listen and watch the teacher.
Listen again and do.

- Take out your check.
- Write the check.
- Show your driver's license.
- Show your credit card.

Write the sentences.

1.

2.

3.

4.

Speak and write about how you pay the rent.

106   UNIT 6

Reduced Student Book
Page 106, Unit 6

PRESENT

1. **Ask questions** about the topic. Use the vocabulary and grammar from the unit, from the TPR activity, or from previous units. For example, in Unit 6 on page 106, ask *When do you pay the rent? Do you pay your rent on the first of the month? Do you write a check?*

MODEL

2. Write **model sentences** on the board or on an overhead transparency using students' answers. Review the information by asking students to **listen and repeat** the sentences.

WRITE

3. Then ask students to **write their own sentences or stories** about the topic. Tell them they can use sentences on the board or overhead transparency that **describe their experience**. Walk around and provide help as necessary.

SHARE

4. Form pairs or small groups. Ask students to take turns **reading** their stories aloud to their partner(s).

Write . . .
Listen . . .

Write Ch and ch.

Ch

ch

Write ch in the words. Read.

___eck   ___ange   wat___

___arge   tea___er   lun___

Write the words in the sentences.

1.

Do you have _____?

2.

I eat _____ at 12:00.

3.

Cash or _____?

4.

Write the _____ for $20.

Listen and repeat the words and the sentences.

104 UNIT 6

Reduced Student Book
Page 104, Unit 6

| PRESENT | 1. **Say** the target letter(s) and sound and have students **repeat chorally**. |

| DEMONSTRATE | 2. Demonstrate **writing the capital and small letters**. Ask students to practice writing the letter(s) in their books. Walk around and provide help as necessary. |

| MODEL | 3. Have students look at the word list in the second exercise. These are **familiar words** from previous lessons. If the words have blanks, write the first incomplete word on the board and demonstrate filling in the target letter. **Model** the word and have students **repeat**. Then have students complete the list and read the words aloud softly. |

4. If the words do not have blanks, **model** the first word and ask students to **repeat**. Then ask students to read the list of words aloud softly to themselves.

| PRACTICE | 5. Ask students to **write the words** in the sentences. Then have them practice reading the sentences aloud softly. |

6. Play the audio CD or say the words and sentences aloud and ask students to **repeat**. Ask students to pay attention to the pronunciation and to focus on **self-correction**. Have students listen and repeat two or three times.

🎧 Listen to the story.

> 🎧 **Listen to the story.**
> **Listen again. Write the numbers 1 to 6.**
>
> [ ] [1]
>
> [5] [ ]
>
> [ ] [3]
>
> 📖 **Read the story.**
>
> **Write the story.**
>
> 1. _____
> 2. _____
> 3. _____
> 4. _____
> 5. _____
> 6. _____
>
> UNIT 6   107

Reduced Student Book
Page 107, Unit 6

PRESENT

1. **Books closed.** Play the audio CD or read the story aloud and **show** students the story flashcards in the correct order as they **listen**. Then display the flashcards in the correct order. For example, put them on the chalk tray, hang them on the wall, or have students hold them in front of the class. Write the sequence number over the card.

CHECK

2. To check comprehension, say the sentences out of order and ask students to **say the picture number** that matches each sentence.

3. Play the audio CD or read the story aloud. Ask students to **listen again and repeat** the story. Point to each flashcard as the students say the sentence that corresponds to it. Have students listen two or three times.

PRACTICE

4. **Books open.** For Units 1-5, ask students to **practice telling the story** to a partner or partners as they point to the pictures.

   For Units 6-10, ask students to listen to the story and write the numbers that show the correct order of the sentences. Form pairs or small groups. Then ask students to take turns **telling the story** as they point to the pictures.

5. Have students turn to the corresponding story page in the Stories section of the Student Book. Ask students to **read the story** by themselves.

6. Ask students to **write the story** in their books. Students can copy the sentences directly from the book if necessary.

Ask your classmates.

Answer the questions.

1. What time do you get up?

   7:00

2. What time do you eat lunch?

   :

3. What time do you go to sleep?

   :

Ask your classmates. Write the times.

	Get Up	Eat Lunch	Go to Sleep
Classmate 1			
Classmate 2			
Classmate 3			

Talk about your classmates.

Kim **gets** up at 8:00.   May and Li **get** up at 7:00.

68   UNIT 4

Reduced Student Book
Page 68, Unit 4

MODEL

1. **Model** the review questions or conversation using your own information. Repeat the questions or conversation two or three times.

DEMONSTRATE

2. Write the questions or the conversation on the board or on an overhead transparency. Ask various students for their information and demonstrate **writing the information** in the blanks. Ask students to write their own information in their books.

DRILL

3. **Repetition Drills**

   • Say each question or conversation line and ask the class to repeat chorally. Use various students' answers during the drill.

   • For conversations, divide the class into two groups: Speaker A and Speaker B. Say each line and ask each group to repeat their lines chorally. Then reverse the groups and repeat the drill.

4. **Question/Answer Drills**

   • Assign roles. The teacher is Speaker A and asks the question(s). The students are Speaker B and answer the question(s).

   • Then reverse roles so that the students ask the questions.

PRACTICE

5. Form two groups: Group A walks around and Group B sits. Have Group A move around the room and **ask questions and write the answers**. Walk around and provide help as needed.

6. Reverse the groups. Group A sits. Have Group B move around the room and **ask questions and write answers**. Walk around and provide help as needed.

Talk about your classmates.

Answer the questions.

1. What time do you get up?

   7:00

2. What time do you eat lunch?

3. What time do you go to sleep?

Ask your classmates. Write the times.

	Get Up	Eat Lunch	Go to Sleep
Classmate 1			
Classmate 2			
Classmate 3			

Talk about your classmates.

Kim **gets** up at 8:00.   May and Li **get** up at 7:00.

68   UNIT 4

Reduced Student Book
Page 68, Unit 4

MODEL

1. Write **example sentences** on the board or on an overhead transparency to model the grammatical structure students will need. Point out the target structure highlighted in bold on the Student Book page.

2. **Say** the sentences and ask students to **repeat** chorally.

VERIFY

3. Call on various students to tell the class one thing they learned about their classmate(s) in the Ask your classmate activity. **Verify the information** by asking if it is correct, for example: *Maria. Lee says you work on Sunday. Do you work on Sunday?*

PRACTICE

4. Form small groups. Have students **take turns talking** about the classmate they talked to in the Ask your classmate activity. Walk around and provide help as necessary.

SUMMARIZE

5. **Summarize the activity** by asking questions. For Units 1-4, ask students to stand up in response to *Yes/No* questions. For example in Unit 2, ask *Can you spell your name? If yes, please stand up.* For Units 5-10, ask questions with *How many students . . . ?* For example, in Unit 5, ask *How many students work on Sunday? Please stand up.*

6. Write **summary sentences** on the board. For example, in Unit 5, write on the board *Six students work on Sunday.* Then ask students to **practice reading** the sentences aloud softly.

Listen and point. Listen again and repeat.

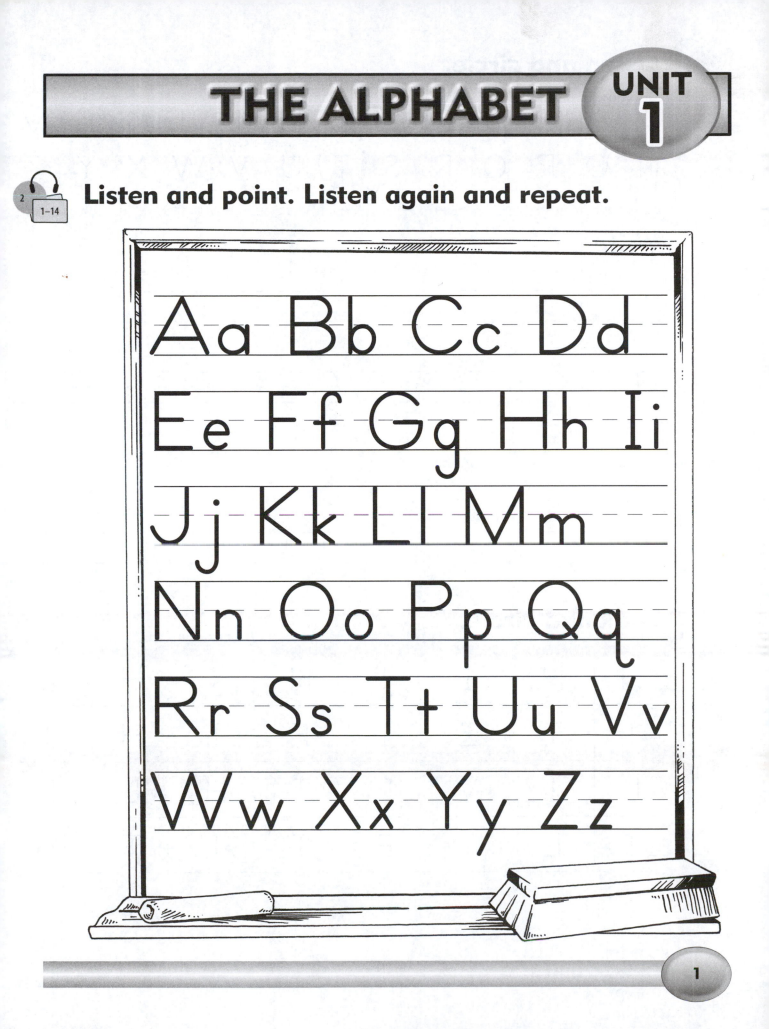

 **Listen and circle.**

A B C D E F G (H) (I) J K (L) M
N O P Q R S (T) U V W X Y Z

Write.

L

T

I

H

Look and circle.

H	(H)	I	T	H	K	H	E
I	I	T	Z	I	F	I	H	I
L	I	V	L	T	H	L	L
T	L	T	F	T	I	T	H

Listen and circle.

A B C D E F G H I J K L M
N O P Q R S T U (V) W X Y Z

Write.

V V

W W

X X

Y Y

Look and circle.

V	(V)	Y	V	W	N	V	U
W	M	W	V	Z	W	W	X
X	Z	K	X	X	Y	H	X
Y	Y	V	Y	X	W	Y	K

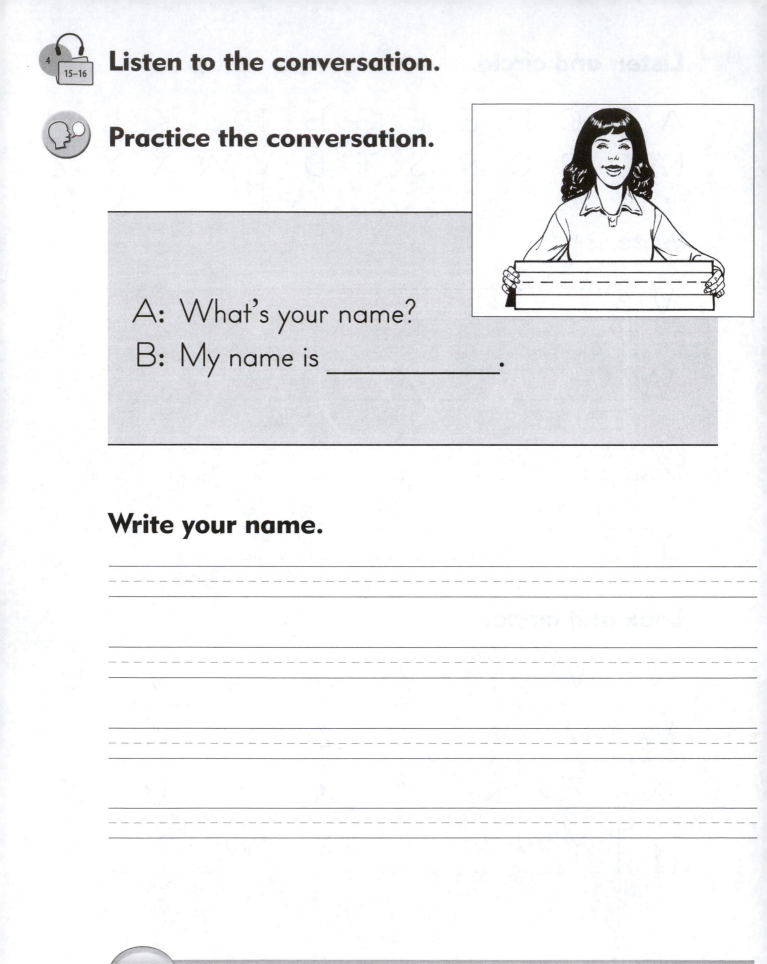

Listen to the conversation.

15–16

Practice the conversation.

A: What's your name?

B: My name is _____.

Write your name.

Listen and circle.

A B C D E F G H I J K L M
N O P Q R S T U V W X Y Z

Write.

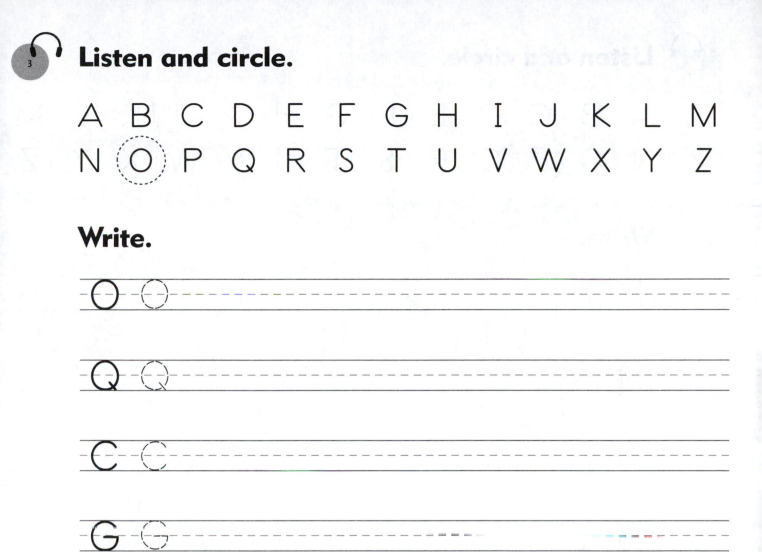

O   O

Q   Q

C   C

G   G

Look and circle.

C	O	C	Q	C	G	L	C
G	G	O	C	G	Q	G	E
O	C	Q	O	G	O	O	S
Q	O	Q	Q	C	Q	G	V

Listen and circle.

A B C D E F G H I J K L M
N O P Q R S T U V W X Y Z

Write.

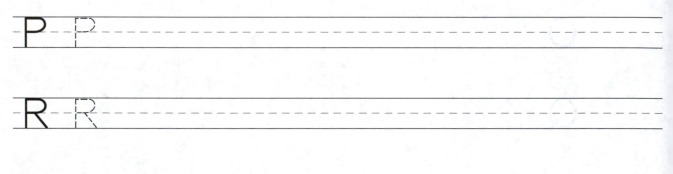

P P

R R

D D

B B

Look and circle.

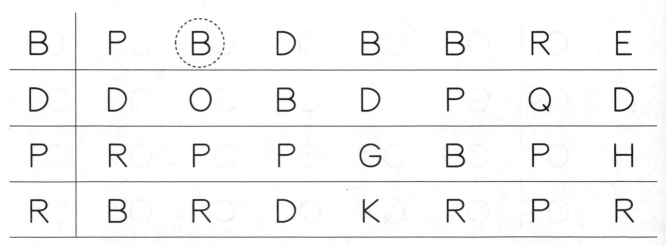

B	P	B	D	B	B	R	E
D	D	O	B	D	P	Q	D
P	R	P	P	G	B	P	H
R	B	R	D	K	R	P	R

Listen to the conversation.

Practice the conversation.

A: What's your first name?

B: My first name is _____.

A: What's your last name?

B: My last name is _____.

Write your name.

First Name _____

Last Name _____

Name _____
First   Last

Name _____ , _____
Last   First

2–8

Write the capital letters.

A A

B B

C C

D D

E E

F F

G G

H H

I I

J J

K K

L L

M M

8–14 **Write the capital letters.**

N N

O O

P P

Q Q

R R

S S

T T

U U

V V

W W

X X

Y Y

Z Z

Listen and circle.

a b c d e f g h i j k l m

n o p q (r) s t u v w x y z

Write.

r r

n n

m m

u u

Look and circle.

m	(m)	u	m	n	m	h	r
n	r	n	n	m	v	n	u
r	n	u	r	c	r	m	r
u	u	v	u	n	y	u	r

Listen and circle.

a b c d e f g (h) i j k l m
n o p q r s t u v w x y z

Write.

h h

b b

t t

f f

Look and circle.

b	(b)	d	h	b	l	b	d
f	t	k	f	f	b	l	f
h	h	b	t	h	n	h	d
t	x	t	f	t	l	k	t

**Listen and watch the teacher.
Listen again and do.**

> ◆ Listen.
>
> ◆ Write an A.
>
> ◆ Say A.
>
> ◆ Circle the A.

Read and circle.

1.

   Say A.

   (Write an A.)

2.

   Listen.

   Circle the A.

3.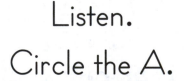

   Circle the A.

   Write an A.

4.

   Say A.

   Listen.

Listen and circle.

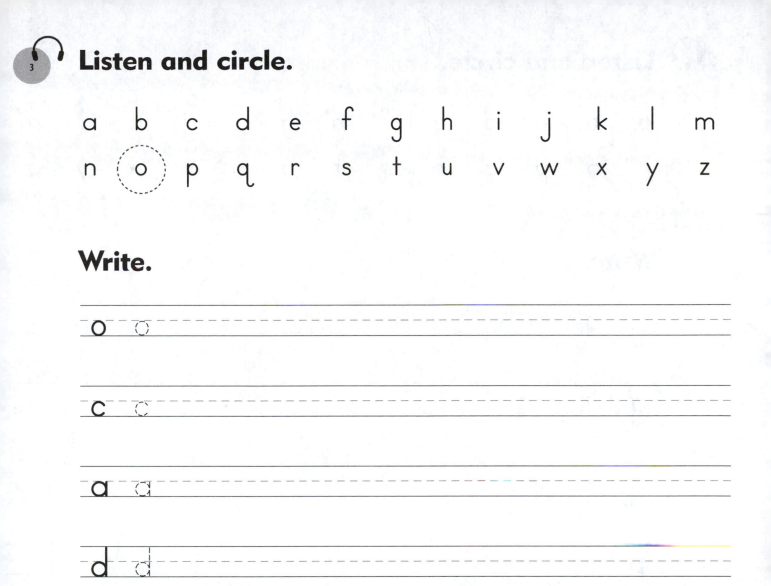

a b c d e f g h i j k l m

n o p q r s t u v w x y z

Write.

o o

c c

a a

d d

Look and circle.

a	d	a	a	o	c	a	b
c	a	o	c	e	c	d	c
d	d	a	d	d	b	o	h
o	b	o	a	p	o	c	o

Listen and circle.

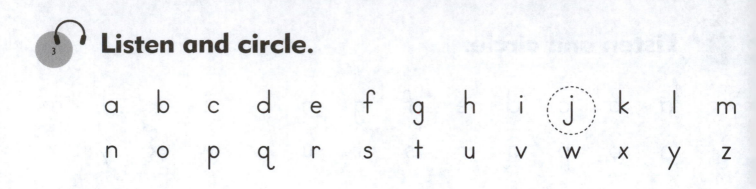

a b c d e f g h i j k l m
n o p q r s t u v w x y z

Write.

j   j

g   g

q   q

p   p

Look and circle.

g	j	g	g	a	q	g	p
j	i	q	j	j	p	g	j
p	p	b	p	q	d	p	g
q	g	q	q	b	j	q	a

Ask a classmate.

A: What's your first name?

B: _____

A: Please spell it.

B: _____

A: What's your last name?

B: _____

A: Please spell it.

B: _____

Write the first name and last name.

	First Name	Last Name
Classmate		

Talk about your classmate.

My classmate's first name is _____.

My classmate's last name is _____.

Write the small letters.

a   a

b   b

c   c

d   d

e   e

f   f

g   g

h   h

i   i

j   j

k   k

l   l

m   m

Write the small letters.

n   n

o   o

p   p

q   q

r   r

s   s

t   t

u   u

v   v

w   w

x   x

y   y

z   z

Look and circle.

Name	(Name)	Mane	(Name)	Mean
First	Four	First	First	Start
Last	Lost	Last	Stall	Last

Write your name.

Name _____

First Name _____

Last Name _____

Name _____ , _____
              Last   First

Name _____
              First   Last

Say the alphabet.

A a   B b   C c   D d   E e   F f   G g
H h   I i   J j   K k   L l   M m   N n
O o   P p   Q q   R r   S s   T t   U u
V v   W w   X x   Y y   Z z

Write the capital letters.

A ___   ___   ___   E ___   ___   ___

___   I ___   ___   ___   ___   ___   N

___   ___   ___   R ___   ___   ___   ___

V ___   ___   ___   ___

Write the small letters.

___   b ___   ___   ___   ___   ___

___   ___   ___   ___   m ___

___   ___   ___   ___   ___

___   ___   y ___

Look and circle.

F	E	f	b	T
Y	j	l	g	y
Q	a	O	q	d
b	B	d	P	a
E	C	G	e	H

Write the capital letters.

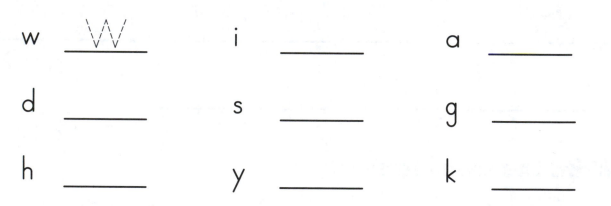

w	W	i	____	a	____
d	____	s	____	g	____
h	____	y	____	k	____

Write the small letters.

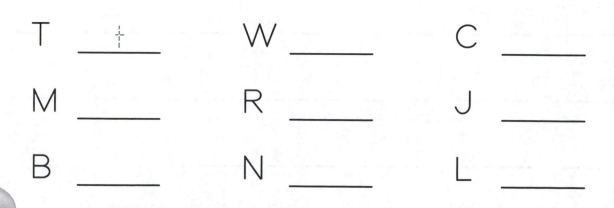

T	t	W	____	C	____
M	____	R	____	J	____
B	____	N	____	L	____

Ask your classmates.

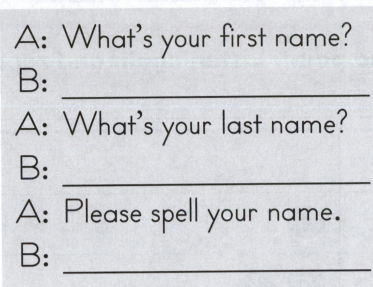

A: What's your first name?

B: _____

A: What's your last name?

B: _____

A: Please spell your name.

B: _____

Write your classmates' names.

First Name	Last Name

Listen and point. Listen again and repeat.

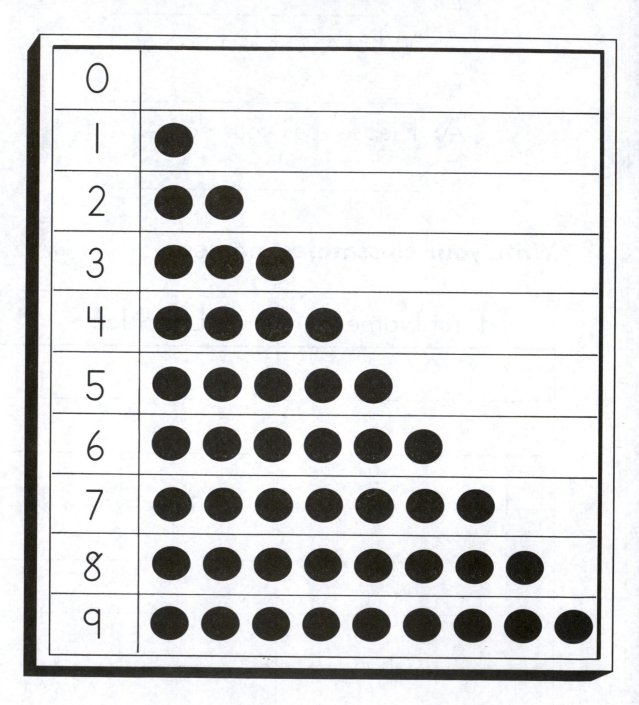

Write the numbers.

0   0

1   1

2   2

3   3

4   4

5   5

6   6

7   7

8   8

9   9

Look and circle.

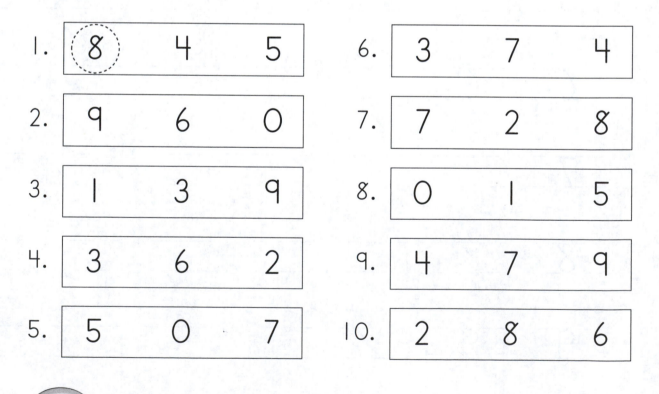

(2) 1 3	3 4 5	8 9 7	0 1 7	8 6 9
5 4 3	6 8 7	5 3 4	6 8 9	2 4 6

Listen and circle.

1. (8)   4   5   6. 3   7   4

2. 9   6   0   7. 7   2   8

3. 1   3   9   8. 0   1   5

4. 3   6   2   9. 4   7   9

5. 5   0   7   10. 2   8   6

Write the numbers.

Listen. Write the phone numbers.

1. 6 2 6 – 7 1 5 3

2. 3 _ 9 – 8 4 _ _

3. 5 _ _ – 0 _ _ 7

4. _ 1 _ – _ _ _ 9

Write your telephone number.

(_____) _____ — _____
Area Code

(_____) _____ — _____
Area Code

Listen to the conversation.

Practice the conversation.

A: What's your phone number?

B: _____

A: Excuse me?

B: _____

Ask your classmates. Write the telephone numbers.

(_____) _____ — _____

(_____) _____ — _____

26   UNIT 2

Write your address.

_____

- -

Number   Street

_____

- -

Number   Street

 Listen to the conversation.

Practice the conversation.

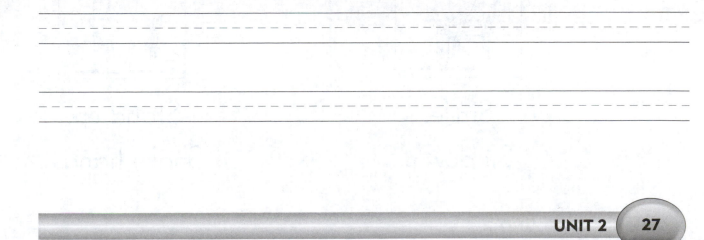

A: What's your address?

B: My address is _____.

A: Excuse me?

B: _____.

Ask your classmates. Write the addresses.

_____

- -

_____

- -

Listen and watch the teacher.

Listen again and do.

> ◆ Stand up.
> ◆ Smile.
> ◆ Shake hands.
> ◆ Sit down.

Read and circle.

1.

   (Smile.)

   Stand up.

2.

   Sit down.

   Shake hands.

3.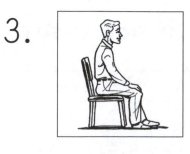

   Smile.

   Sit down.

4.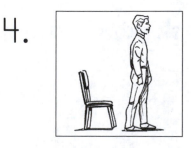

   Stand up.

   Shake hands.

Listen to the conversation.

 Practice the conversation.

A: Hello.
B: Hello.
A: How are you?
B: Fine, thank you.

Write your answers.

1. What's your name?

   _____

2. What's your address?

   _____

3. What's your phone number?

   (_____) _____ — _____

Ask your classmates.

Write the capital S and small s.

S

s

Write s in the words. Read.

_s_ay   _tand

_it   _mile

Write the words.

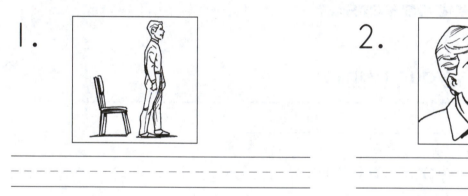

1.

2.

3.

4.

Listen to the teacher and repeat the words.

Say the words.

city

state

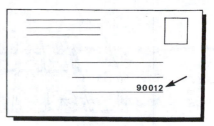

zip code

Say your city, state, and zip code.

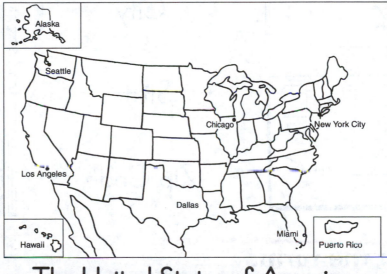

The United States of America

Write.

1. Write your city. _____

2. Write your state. _____

3. Write your zip code. _____

Match.

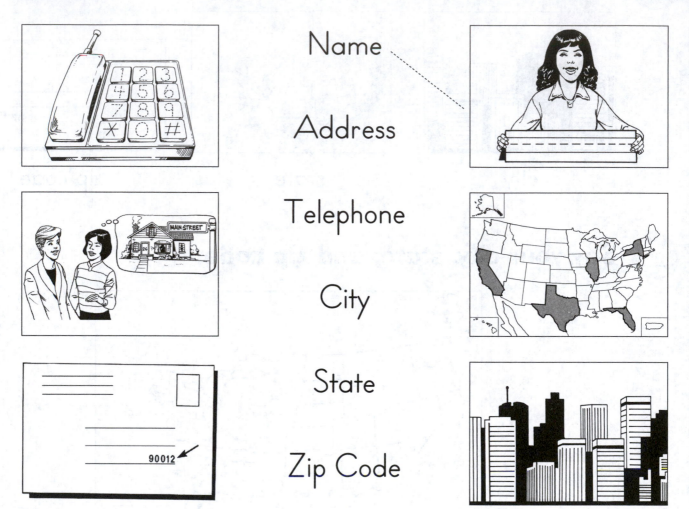

Name

Address

Telephone

City

State

Zip Code

Fill out the form.

Name _____
　　　　　　　　First　　　　　　　　　　　　　　Last

Address _____

City _____ State _____

Zip Code _____ Telephone (_____) _____

Ask your classmates.

A: What's your address?

B: _____

A: Please write it.

B: OK. Here you are.

A: Thank you.

Write the information.

	Address
Classmate 1	
Classmate 2	
Classmate 3	
Classmate 4	

 **Talk about your classmates.**

Mario**'s** address is _____.

Write to your teacher.

Name _____

Address _____

City   State   Zip Code

STAMP

Name _____

Address _____

City   State   Zip Code

Write to a classmate.

_____

_____

_____

STAMP

_____

_____

_____

Listen to the story.

1.

2.

3.

4.

Read the story.

Write the story.

1.

2.

3.

4.

Answer the questions. Use a check (✓).

1. Do you go to school?

☑ Yes, I do.

☐ No, I don't.

2. Do you go to work?

☐ Yes, I do.

☐ No, I don't.

3. Do you study English?

☐ Yes, I do.

☐ No, I don't.

4. Do you walk home?

☐ Yes, I do.

☐ No, I don't.

 Ask a classmate.

Write the capital N and small n.

N ⎯ ⎯ ⎯ ⎯ ⎯ ⎯ ⎯ ⎯

n ⎯ ⎯ ⎯ ⎯ ⎯ ⎯ ⎯ ⎯

Write n in the words. Read.

__n_ame   ___o

___umber   dow___

Write the words in the sentences.

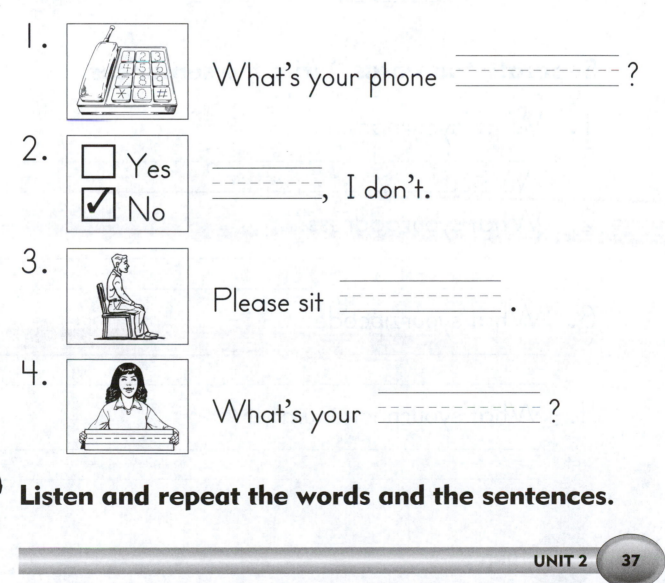

1. What's your phone _____ ?

2. □ Yes
   ☑ No   _____ , I don't.

3. Please sit _____ .

4. What's your _____ ?

Listen and repeat the words and the sentences.

Circle the word or words.

1. name — m a n a m e n e
2. phone — e p h o n e h o n p h
3. address — d e s a d d r e s s e
4. city — c i t c i t y c y t i y
5. state — e s t a t a t s t a t e
6. zip code — p z i p d o z c o d e t

Separate the words. Write the sentences.

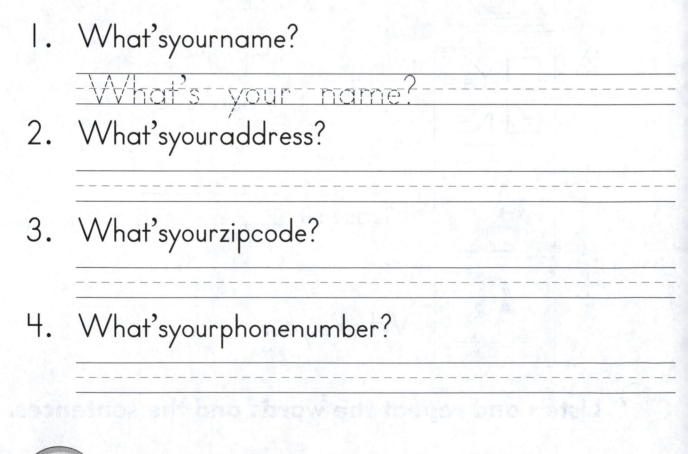

1. What'syourname?

   What's your name?

2. What'syouraddress?

3. What'syourzipcode?

4. What'syourphonenumber?

14 **Listen and repeat.**

s	n
say	name
sit	number
stand	no
school	down
study	phone
address	listen

15 **Listen and write** s **or** n.
Listen again and repeat.

1. I go to ⎯school.

2. I ⎯tudy English.

3. Liste⎯ to the teacher.

4. Please ⎯it dow⎯.

5. What'⎯ your pho⎯e ⎯umber?

Fill out the form.

Name _____ , _____
                  Last   First

Address _____
              Number   Street

_____
      City   State   Zip Code

Phone number (_____)_____

Ask your classmates.

A: What's your area code?

B: _____

A: What's your phone number?

B: _____

Write the numbers.

	Area Code	Phone Number
Classmate 1		
Classmate 2		

Talk about your classmates.

Carla**'s** phone number is _____.

Listen and point. Listen again and repeat.

1. clock	2. board	3. calendar	4. chair	5. desk
6. book	7. pencil	8. paper	9. student	10. teacher

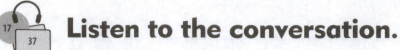 **Listen to the conversation.**

Practice the conversation.

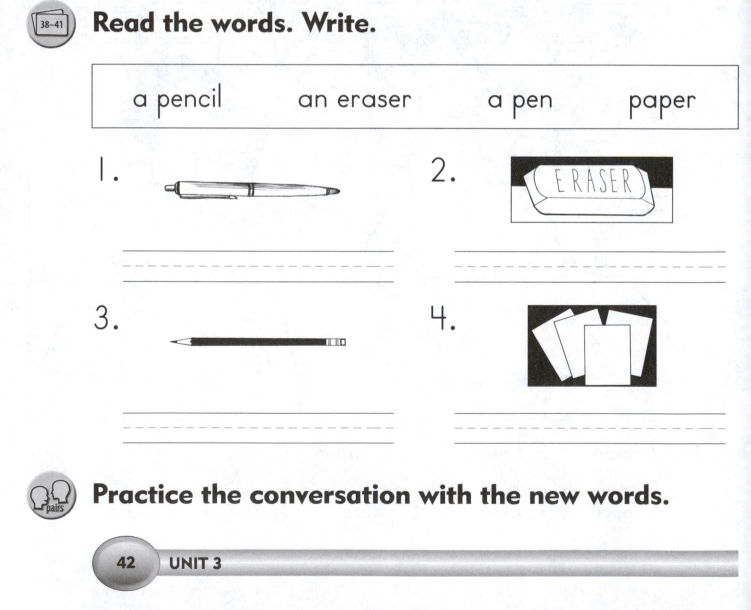

A: Excuse me. I need <u>a pencil</u>.
B: OK. Here you are.
A: Thank you very much.
B: You're welcome.

38–41 **Read the words. Write.**

| a pencil | an eraser | a pen | paper |

1.

2.

3.

4.

Practice the conversation with the new words.

Listen and watch the teacher.
Listen again and do.

♦ Open the book.
♦ Turn to page 5.
♦ Write with a pencil.
♦ Close the book.

Read and circle.

1.

Close the book.
Turn to page 5.

2.

Sit down.
Close the book.

3.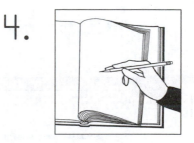

Open the book.
Shake hands.

4.

Write with a pencil.
Write on the board.

((●)) **Write P and p.**

P

p

Write p in the words. Read.

__encil   __age   stand u__

__a__er   o__en   __en

Write the words in the sentences.

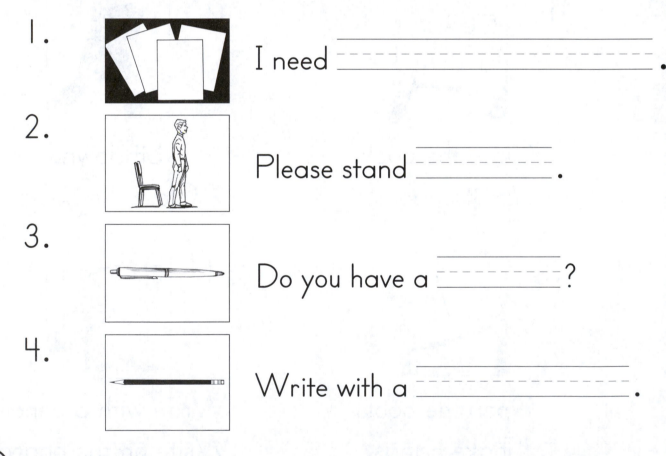

1.   I need _____ .

2.   Please stand _____ .

3.   Do you have a _____ ?

4.   Write with a _____ .

🎧 **Listen and repeat the words and the sentences.**

18

🎧 19 42 Listen to the conversation.

🗣 Practice the conversation.

A: Excuse me. Where's the <u>school</u>?
B: It's over there.
A: Where's the <u>office</u>?
B: Sorry. I don't know.

📇 43–46 Read the words. Write.

office	classroom	cafeteria	library

1.

_ _ _ _ _ _ _ _ _ _ _ _ _ _

2.

_ _ _ _ _ _ _ _ _ _ _ _ _ _

3.

_ _ _ _ _ _ _ _ _ _ _ _ _ _

4.

_ _ _ _ _ _ _ _ _ _ _ _ _ _

👥 pairs Practice the conversation with the new words.

Read.

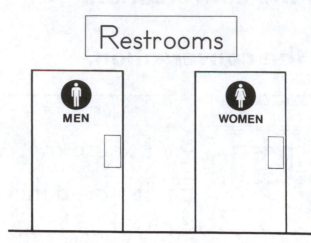

Circle the word.

MEN   WOMEN

MEN   WOMEN

Write.

_____

_____

 Practice the conversation.

A: Excuse me. Where's the restroom?

B: It's over there.

Walk around the school.
Check (✓) Open **or** Closed.

	Open	Closed
1. Classroom	✓	
2. Cafeteria		
3. Library		
4. Office		
5. Men's Restroom		
6. Women's Restroom		

Write sentences like this.

1. The classroom is open.

2.

3.

4.

5.

6.

Tell your class about your school.

Write C and c.

C _____

c _____

Write c in the words. Read.

__alendar   __lock   wel__ome

__lassroom   __afeteria   __lose

Write the words in the sentences.

1.   Please _____ your book.

2.   Where's the _____ ?

3.   The _____ is over there.

4.   The _____ is open.

🎧 **Listen and repeat the words and the sentences.**

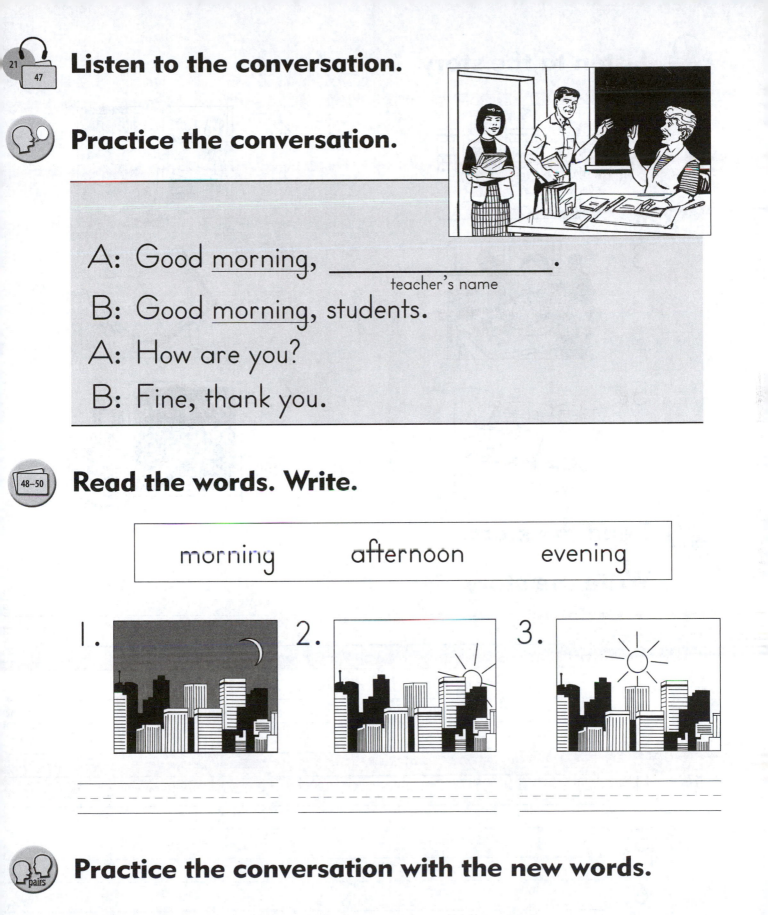

Listen to the conversation.

Practice the conversation.

A: Good <u>morning</u>, _____.
teacher's name

B: Good <u>morning</u>, students.

A: How are you?

B: Fine, thank you.

Read the words. Write.

| morning | afternoon | evening |

1. _____

2. _____

3. _____

Practice the conversation with the new words.

Listen to the story.

1.    2.

3.   4.

5.    6.

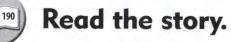

Read the story.

Write the story.

1. _____

2. _____

3. _____

4. _____

5. _____

6. _____

Listen to the conversation.

 Practice the conversation.

A: Are you a student?

B: Yes. I study English.

A: Where do you study?

B: At _____.

A: When is your class?

B: In the _____.

Answer the questions. Write In the morning, In the afternoon, **or** In the evening.

1. When do you go to work?

2. When do you go to school?

3. When do you go home?

4. When do you study English?

 Ask a classmate.

Write W and w.

W _____ _____

w _____ _____

Write w in the words. Read.

__ork   __elcome   __omen   __here

__alk   t__elve   __hat   __hen

Write the words in the sentences.

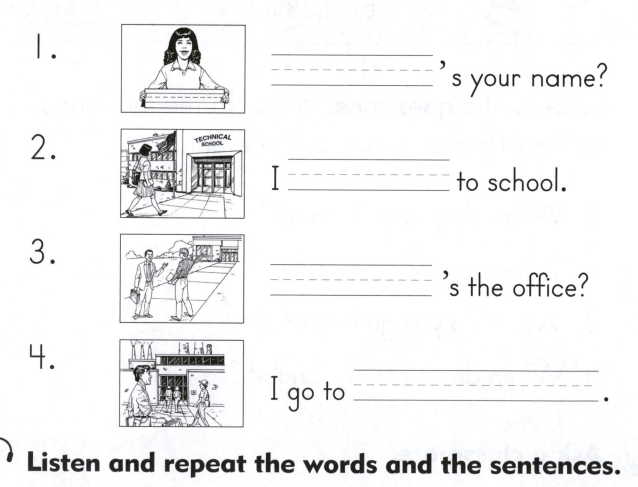

1. _____'s your name?

2. I _____ to school.

3. _____'s the office?

4. I go to _____.

Listen to the conversation.

 **Practice the conversation.**

A: Do you study English?

B: Yes, I do.

A: Where's your class?

B: It's in Room _____.

A: When's your class?

B: In the _____.

Fill out the form.

Name of Student _____

Name of Teacher _____

Name of School _____

School Address _____
                                              Street

_____
City   State   Zip Code

School Telephone (_____) _____

Class _____ Room Number _____

 **Tell your class about your school.**

Find and circle the words.

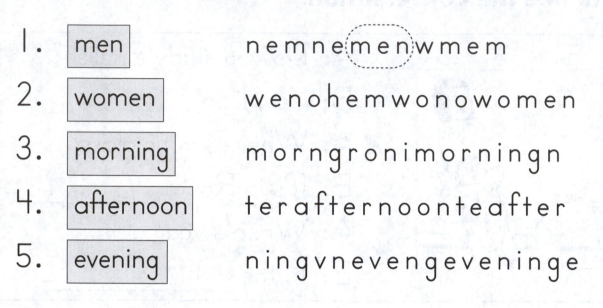

1. men   n e m n e m e n w m e m

2. women   w e n o h e m w o n o w o m e n

3. morning   m o r n g r o n i m o r n i n g n

4. afternoon t e r a f t e r n o o n t e a f t e r

5. evening   n i n g v n e v e n g e v e n i n g e

Separate the words. Write the sentences.

1. Ineedapencil.
   _____

2. Thankyouverymuch.
   _____

3. DoyoustudyEnglish?
   _____

4. Openthebook.
   _____

Listen and repeat.

p	c	w
pencil	calendar	work
page	cafeteria	walk
paper	come	women
open	clock	what
stand up	classroom	where
zip code	close	when

Write p, c, or w. Read.

1. I ____alk to ____ork.

2. Turn to ____age 5.

3. The ____lassroom is ____losed.

4. I need a ____encil and ____a____er.

5. ____ere's the ____omen's restroom?

Write one word in each box.

calendar	clock	pencil	desk	classroom
cafeteria	book	paper	eraser	restroom
library	office	chair	board	pen

Listen. Write an ✕ on the word your teacher says. The students with all ✕s win.

Listen and watch the teacher.
Listen again and repeat.

Listen to the conversation.

 **Practice the conversation.**

A: What time is it?

B: It's <u>6:00</u>.

A: Thank you.

B: You're welcome.

Use the clock on page 57 to show the time.
Say the time.

1.   5:00   6. 12:00

2.   3:00   7.   8:00

3.   9:00   8.   4:00

4.   1:00   9. 10:00

5. 11:00   10.   7:00

Practice the conversation using the times.

Write T and t.

T ⎯ ⎯ ⎯ ⎯ ⎯ ⎯

t ⎯ ⎯ ⎯ ⎯ ⎯ ⎯

Write t in the words. Read.

__ime   __urn   wri__e

__elephone   __eacher   si__

Write the words in the sentences.

1. Please ⎯⎯⎯⎯⎯⎯ down.

2. What's your ⎯⎯⎯⎯⎯⎯ number?

3. What ⎯⎯⎯⎯⎯⎯ is it?

4. Please ⎯⎯⎯⎯⎯⎯ your name.

Listen and repeat the words and the sentences.

Listen to the teacher. Repeat the numbers. Write.

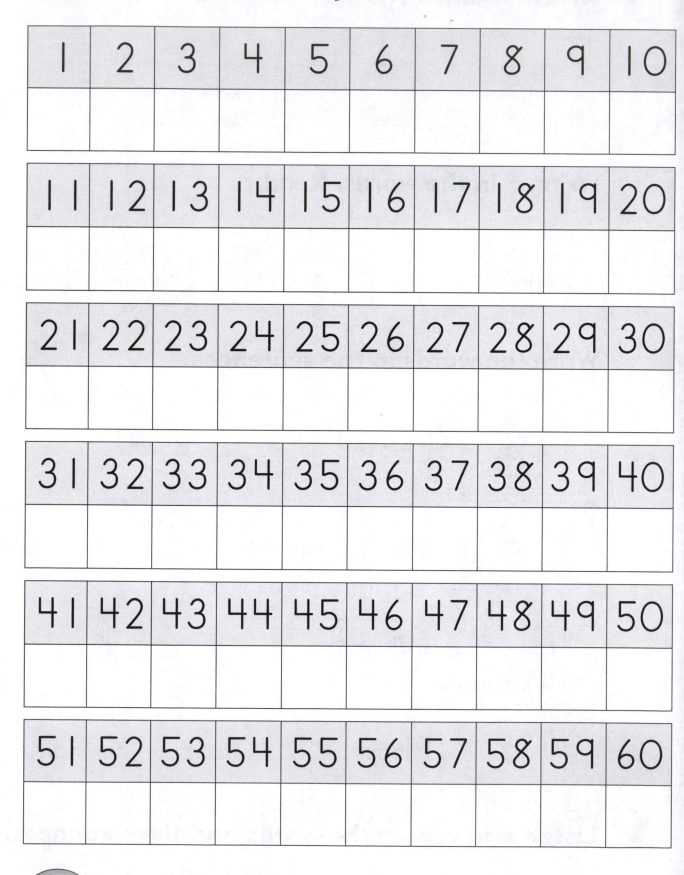

1	2	3	4	5	6	7	8	9	10

11	12	13	14	15	16	17	18	19	20

21	22	23	24	25	26	27	28	29	30

31	32	33	34	35	36	37	38	39	40

41	42	43	44	45	46	47	48	49	50

51	52	53	54	55	56	57	58	59	60

Write the minutes.

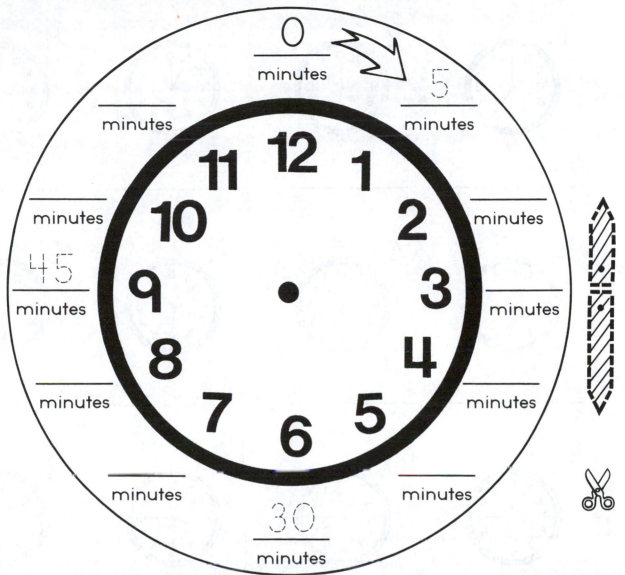

Use the clock. Say the time.

Hour : Minutes

1:15   It's one fifteen.

9:30   It's nine thirty.

3:45   It's three forty-five.

7:00   It's seven o'clock.

Say and write the time.

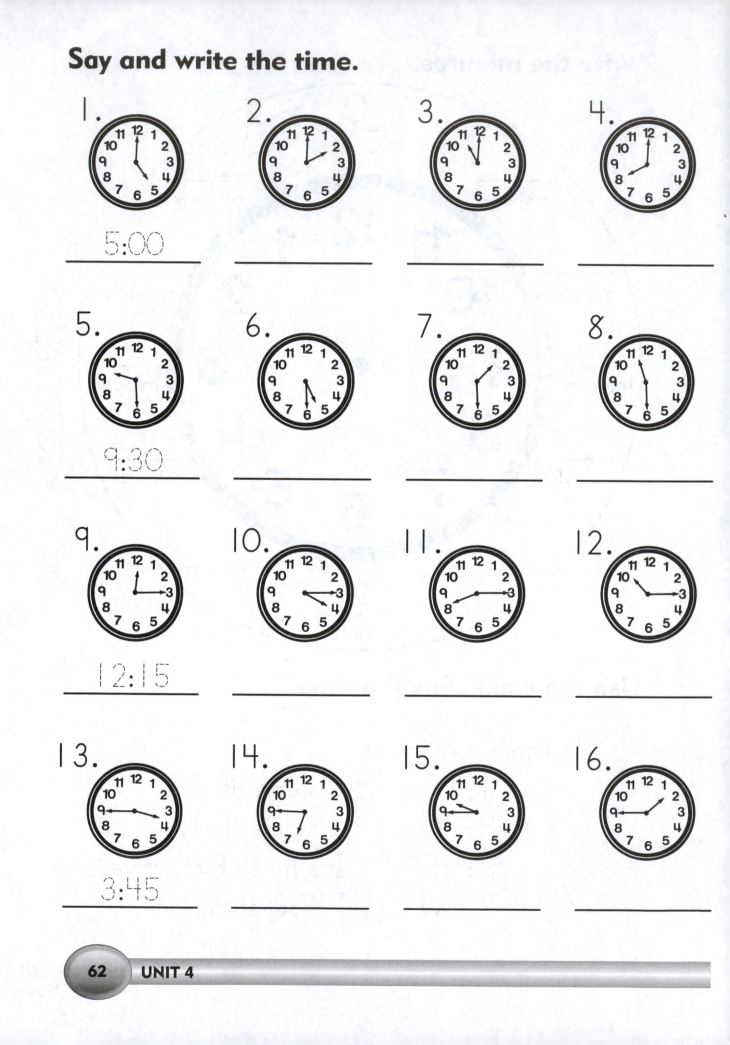

1. 5:00

2. _____

3. _____

4. _____

5. 9:30

6. _____

7. _____

8. _____

9. 12:15

10. _____

11. _____

12. _____

13. 3:45

14. _____

15. _____

16. _____

Listen to the conversation.

Practice the conversation.

A: Goodbye, _____.
　　　　　　　　　　　teacher's name

B: Goodbye, everyone.

A: See you tomorrow.

B: Remember, class starts at _____.
　　　　　　　　　　　　　　　　　　time

　　Please come on time!

Draw the time. Say the time.

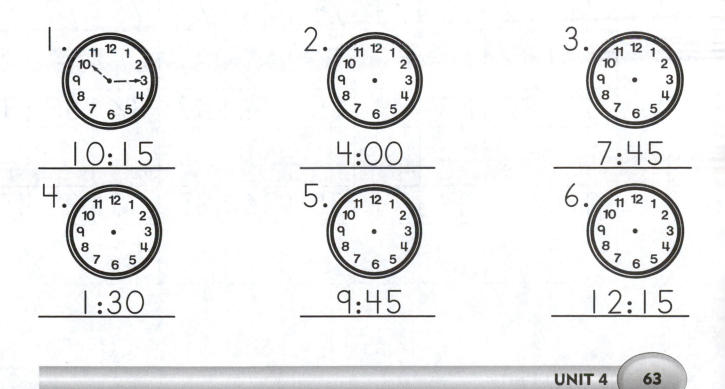

1. 10:15

2. 4:00

3. 7:45

4. 1:30

5. 9:45

6. 12:15

Say and write the missing numbers.

1	2		4	5	6		8	9	
	12	13	14		16	17	18		20
21		23		25	26	27		29	30
31	32		34	35	36		38	39	
41		43	44	45		47	48		50
	52	53	54		56	57		59	60

Listen to the teacher. Repeat the numbers. Write.

61	62	63	64	65	66	67	68	69	70
71	72	73	74	75	76	77	78	79	80
81	82	83	84	85	86	87	88	89	90
91	92	93	94	95	96	97	98	99	100

31 **Listen and repeat the numbers. Then write.**

13	thirteen	thirteen
14	fourteen	
15	fifteen	
16	sixteen	
17	seventeen	
18	eighteen	
19	nineteen	

32 **Listen and repeat the numbers. Then write.**

20	twenty	twenty
30	thirty	
40	forty	
50	fifty	
60	sixty	
70	seventy	
80	eighty	
90	ninety	

Listen and watch the teacher.
Listen again and do.

- ◆ Look at your watch.
- ◆ Look at the clock.
- ◆ Say the time.
- ◆ Write the time.

Read and circle.

1.

Look at the clock.

Look at your watch.

2.

Say the time.

Write the time.

3.

Say the time.

Look at the clock.

4.

Write the time.

Look at your watch.

33 62–67 **Listen to the story.**

1.

2.

3.

4.

5.

6.

191 **Read the story.**

Write the story.

1. _____

2. _____

3. _____

4. _____

5. _____

6. _____

Answer the questions.

1. What time do you get up?

7:00

2. What time do you eat lunch?

  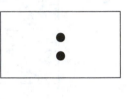

:

3. What time do you go to sleep?

  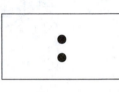

:

 Ask your classmates. Write the times.

	Get Up	Eat Lunch	Go to Sleep
Classmate 1			
Classmate 2			
Classmate 3			

 Talk about your classmates.

Kim **gets** up at 8:00.   May and Li **get** up at 7:00.

Listen to the conversation.

Practice the conversation.

A: When is the <u>bank</u> open?

B: From <u>10</u> to <u>3</u>.

A: Excuse me. What time?

B: It opens at <u>10:00</u>.

It closes at <u>3:00</u>.

Read the words. Write.

restaurant	post office	supermarket

1. _____ _ _ _ _ _ _ _

2. _____ _ _ _ _ _ _ _

3. _____ _ _ _ _ _ _ _

 Practice the conversation with the new words.

Write G **and** g.

G _____

g _____

Write go, get up, **and** goodbye.

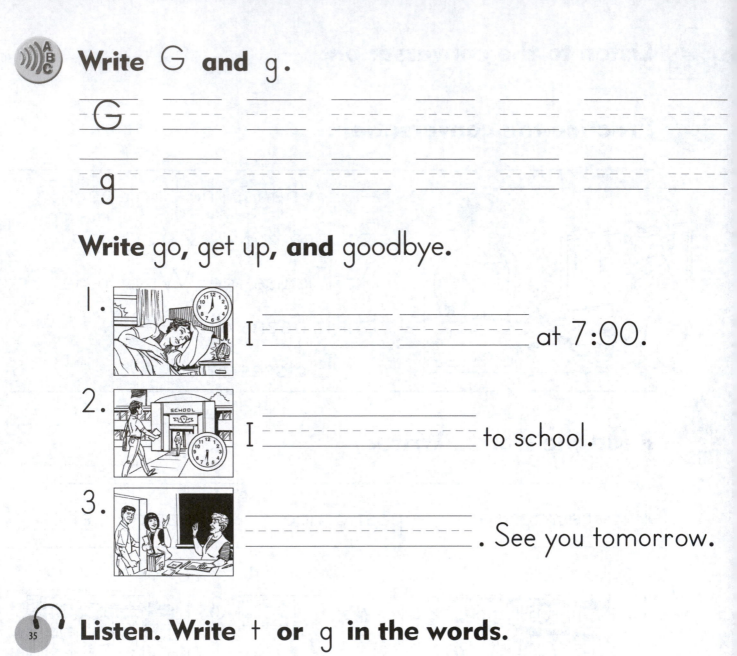

1. I _____ _____ at 7:00.

2. I _____ to school.

3. _____. See you tomorrow.

Listen. Write t **or** g **in the words.**

1. __omorrow

2. __et

3. __ood

4. __ime

5. marke__

6. __oodbye

7. __o

8. ge__

Listen and repeat the sentences and the words.

Write your answers.

1. When do you eat lunch?

   From _____ to _____.

2. When do you work?

   From _____ to _____.

Fill out the form.

Name _____

First   Last

Address _____

_____

City   State   Zip Code

Telephone (_____) _____

	From	To
Work		
Eat lunch		
Study English		
Watch TV		
Sleep		

 Ask your classmates.

When do you _____?

Circle the word.

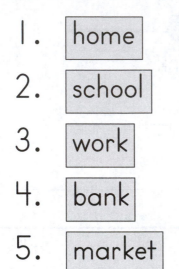

1. home   o m h o e (h o m e) o
2. school   o o s c h o o l c h
3. work   w o k o r w o r k r
4. bank   k a n b a n k a b n
5. market   m a r k e t m a k e t

Separate the words. Write the sentences.

1. Whattimeisit?

   _____

   -

2. Whattimedoyougotoschool?

   _____

   -

3. Whattimedoyougotowork?

   _____

   -

4. Whattimedoyougohome?

   _____

   -

Match.

1. I get up
2. I go to sleep
3. I watch TV
4. I work
5. I study English
6. I go to the bank

 in the morning.

 in the afternoon.

 in the evening.

Ask your classmates.

A: When do you go to the <u>bank</u>?

B: In the _____.

Write morning, afternoon, **or** evening.

	Bank	Market	Post Office
Classmate 1			
Classmate 2			
Classmate 3			

Talk about your classmates.

Ming **goes** to the bank in the afternoon.

Write one number in each box.

11	14	17	20	50
12	15	18	30	60
13	16	19	40	100

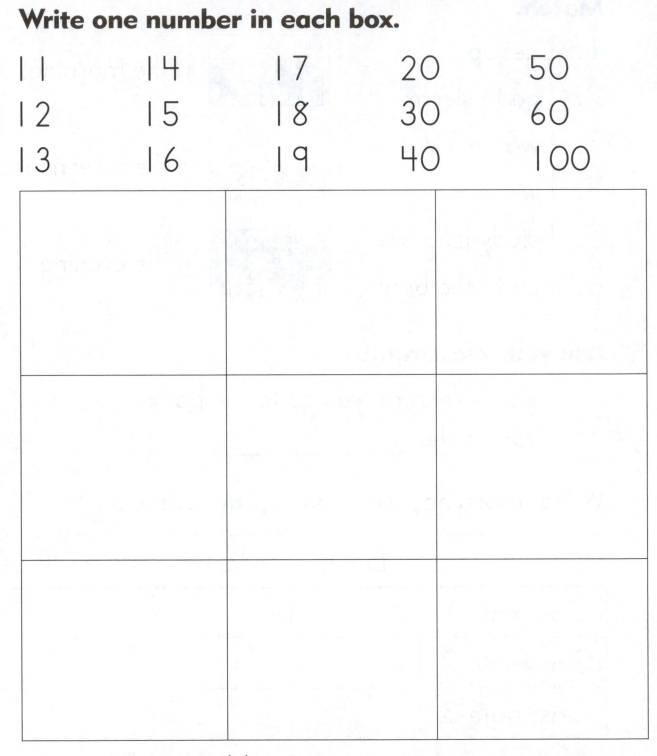

Listen. Write an X on the number your teacher says. The students with all Xs win.

THE CALENDAR

37 **72** **Listen and point. Listen again and repeat.**

OCTOBER

SUNDAY	MONDAY	TUESDAY	WEDNESDAY	THURSDAY	FRIDAY	SATURDAY
1	2	3	4	5	6	7
8	9	10	11	12	13	14
15	16	17	18	19	20	21
22	23	24	25	26	27	28
29	30	31				

Match.

Days of the week

Sunday	Tues.
Monday	Mon.
Tuesday	Wed.
Wednesday	Sun.
Thursday	Sat.
Friday	Thurs.
Saturday	Fri.

Write the words.

1. Fri.   Friday _____
2. Mon.   _____
3. Thurs. _____
4. Sun.   _____
5. Tues.   _____
6. Sat.   _____
7. Wed.   _____

Listen to the conversation.

Practice the conversation.

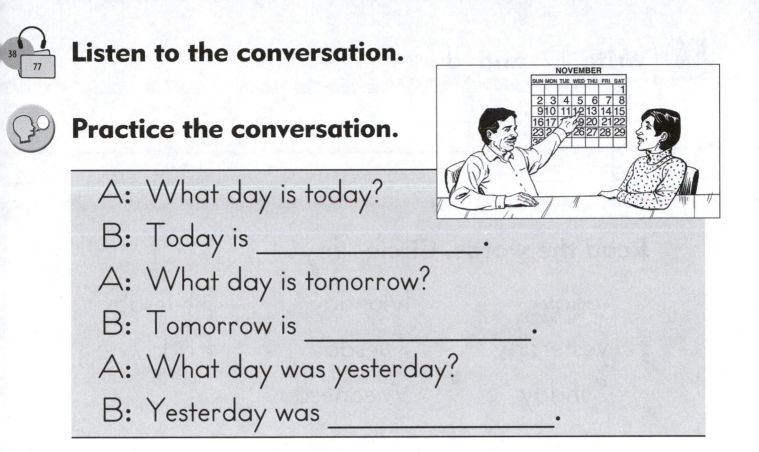

A: What day is today?

B: Today is _____.

A: What day is tomorrow?

B: Tomorrow is _____.

A: What day was yesterday?

B: Yesterday was _____.

Write the days.

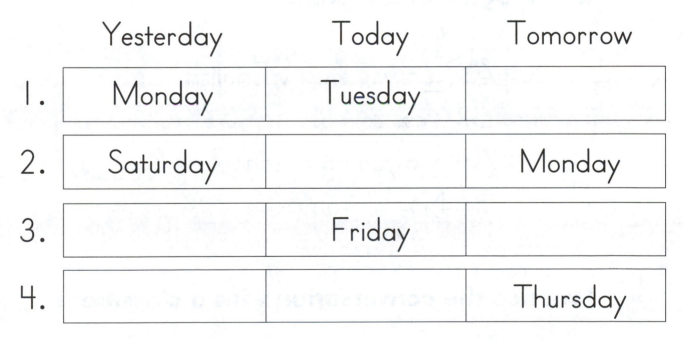

	Yesterday	Today	Tomorrow
1.	Monday	Tuesday	
2.	Saturday		Monday
3.		Friday	
4.			Thursday

Write D **and** d .

D

d

Read the words. Circle day .

today   Monday   Thursday

yesterday   Tuesday   Friday

Sunday   Wednesday

 Listen. Write capital D **or small** d .
Listen again and repeat.

> A: __o you stu__y English?
>
> B: Yes, I __o.
>
> A: __o you go to school on Sun__ay?
>
> B: No, I __on't.

 Practice the conversation with a classmate.

**Listen and watch the teacher.
Listen again and do.**

♦ Come here.

♦ Take a card.

♦ Line up.

♦ Read the card.

Write the sentences.

1.  _____

2.  _____

3.  _____

4.  _____

Ask your classmates.

A: When do you work?

B: _____ to _____.

A: Do you work on Sunday?

B: _____

A: Do you work on Thursday?

B: _____

Write yes **or** no.

	Sun.	Mon.	Tues.	Wed.	Thurs.	Fri.	Sat.
Classmate 1							
Classmate 2							
Classmate 3							
Classmate 4							

Talk about your classmates.

Ahmed **works** Monday to Friday.

Maria and Salina **work** on Saturday and Sunday.

Listen and repeat.

Months of the year

January	February	March
April	May	June
July	August	September
October	November	December

Write the months.

1. June   ~~June~~
2. Oct.   ~~October~~
3. Mar.   _____
4. July   _____
5. Apr.   _____
6. Dec.   _____

7. Aug.   _____
8. Jan.   _____
9. May   _____
10. Nov. _____
11. Feb. _____
12. Sept. _____

Take a month card from your teacher.

Show your card to your classmates.
Line up in order.
Say the month on your card.

Listen to the teacher. Repeat the ordinal numbers.

OCTOBER

SUNDAY	MONDAY	TUESDAY	WEDNESDAY	THURSDAY	FRIDAY	SATURDAY
1 first	2 second	3 third	4 fourth	5 fifth	6 sixth	7 seventh
8 eighth	9 ninth	10 tenth	11 eleventh	12 twelfth	13 thirteenth	14 fourteenth
15 fifteenth	16 sixteenth	17 seventeenth	18 eighteenth	19 nineteenth	20 twentieth	21 twenty-first
22 twenty-second	23 twenty-third	24 twenty-fourth	25 twenty-fifth	26 twenty-sixth	27 twenty-seventh	28 twenty-eighth
29 twenty-ninth	30 thirtieth	31 thirty-first				

Listen to the conversation.

Practice the conversation.

A: What day is today?

B: Today is _____.

A: What's today's date?

B: It's _____ _____.

Write the year.

1. This year is _____.

2. Last year was _____.

3. Next year is _____.

Write the date.

1. Today is _____ _____, _____.
   <u>Month</u>   <u>Day</u>   <u>Year</u>

2. Tomorrow is _____ _____, _____.
   <u>Month</u>   <u>Day</u>   <u>Year</u>

3. Yesterday was _____ _____, _____.
   <u>Month</u>   <u>Day</u>   <u>Year</u>

Listen to the conversation.

Practice the conversation.

A: Where are you from?

B: I was born in _____.
                              country

A: When is your birthday?

B: It's in _____.
                  month

43 **Listen and write the numbers.**
Listen again and repeat.

1. October __12__, 1978

2. March _____, 2006

3. August 22, 19_____

4. December 1, 20_____

5. February _____, 1988

6. November 23, 20_____

Write Y **and** y.

Y

y

Read. Circle the words beginning with Y **or** y.

A: Was yesterday your birthday?

B: Yes, it was.

A: How old are you?

B: I'm 30 years old.

A: Happy birthday!

Write the words beginning with Y **or** y.

1. _____
2. _____
3. _____
4. _____
5. _____

Listen and repeat the conversation and the words.

Listen to the story.

1.  Sun.

2.  Mon.

3. Tues. Thurs.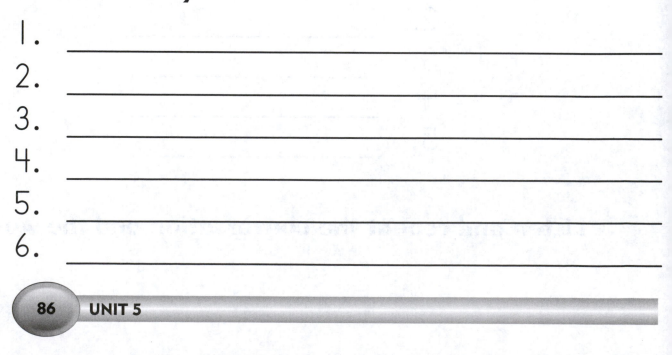

4. Wed.

5. Fri.

6. Sat.

192

Read the story.

Write the story.

1. _____
2. _____
3. _____
4. _____
5. _____
6. _____

Write your answers to the questions.

1.  When do you go shopping?

   I go shopping on _____.
   day

2.  When do you clean the house?

   I clean the house on _____.

3.  When do you eat at a restaurant?

   I eat at a restaurant on _____.

4.  When do you do the laundry?

   I do the _____ on _____.

5.  When do you study English?

   I _____ English on _____.

6.  When do you go to the bank?

   I _____ to the _____ on _____.

 Ask a classmate.

Write Th and th.

Th ─ ─ ─ ─ ─ ─ ─

th ─ ─ ─ ─ ─ ─ ─

46 **Listen and repeat.**

thank you	birthday	fourth	sixth
Thursday	month	fifth	seventh

47 **Listen. Write d, y, or th.**
Listen again and repeat.

1. ___ate
2. ___es
3. ___ank
4. ___esterday

5. four___
6. to___ay
7. mon___
8. ___ear

Fill out the form.

Date _____

Last Name _____ First Name _____

Birthdate _____ _____ , *****
             Month   Day   Year

Make a calendar for this month.

_____

Month and Year

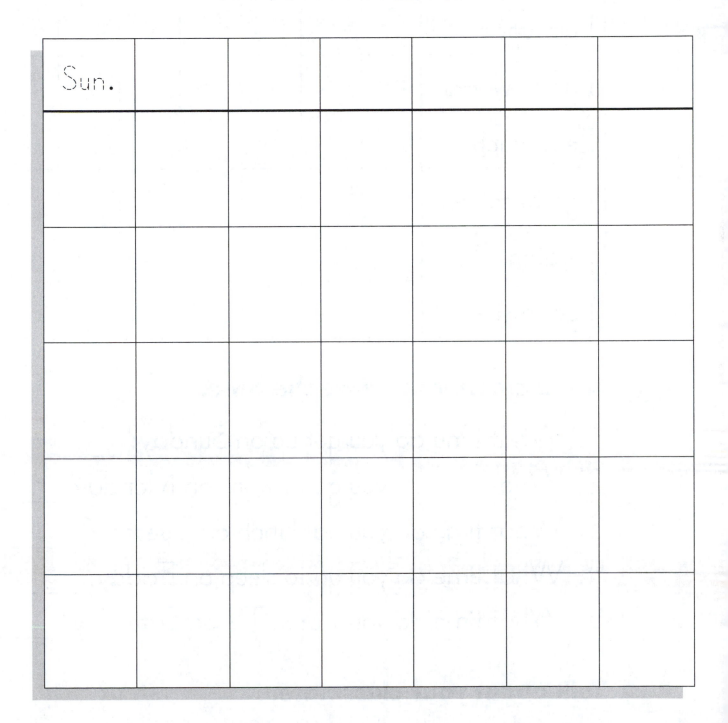

Sun.						

Write the time.

	Sun.	Mon.	Tues.	Wed.	Thurs.	Fri.	Sat.
I get up.							
I go to work.							
I eat lunch.							
I go to school.							
I watch TV.							
I go to sleep.							

Ask a classmate. Write the time.

1. What time do you get up on Sunday? ____

2. What time do you go to work on Monday? ____

3. What time do you eat lunch on Tuesday? ____

4. What time do you go to sleep on Friday? ____

5. What time do you watch TV on Saturday? ____

Talk about your classmate.

Ana **eats** lunch at 12:30 on Tuesday.

Separate the words. Write the sentences.

1. DoyougotoschoolonTuesday?

   _____

2. DoyougotoworkonTuesday?

   _____

3. DoyougoshoppingonTuesday?

   _____

Ask your classmates. Write yes **or** no.

	Tuesday		
	School	Work	Shopping
Classmate 1			
Classmate 2			
Classmate 3			

Talk about your classmates.

Lee **goes** to work on Tuesday.

Linda **doesn't go** to work on Tuesday.

Ask your classmates.

What month is your birthday?

Write the names in the birthday calendar.

January	February	March
_____	_____	_____
_____	_____	_____
_____	_____	_____
April	May	June
_____	_____	_____
_____	_____	_____
_____	_____	_____
July	August	September
_____	_____	_____
_____	_____	_____
_____	_____	_____
October	November	December
_____	_____	_____
_____	_____	_____
_____	_____	_____

Sing "Happy Birthday."

Listen and point. Listen again and repeat.

1. fifty dollars   2. twenty dollars   3. ten dollars   4. five dollars   5. one dollar

6. quarter   7. dime   8. nickel   9. penny

Read the words. Write the numbers.

penny
_____1_____ ¢

nickel
_____5_____ ¢

dime
_____ ¢

quarter
_____ ¢

half-dollar
_____ ¢

one dollar
$ ___1.00___

five dollars
$ _____

ten dollars
$ _____

Add the money.

Dollars	Cents	Dollars and Cents
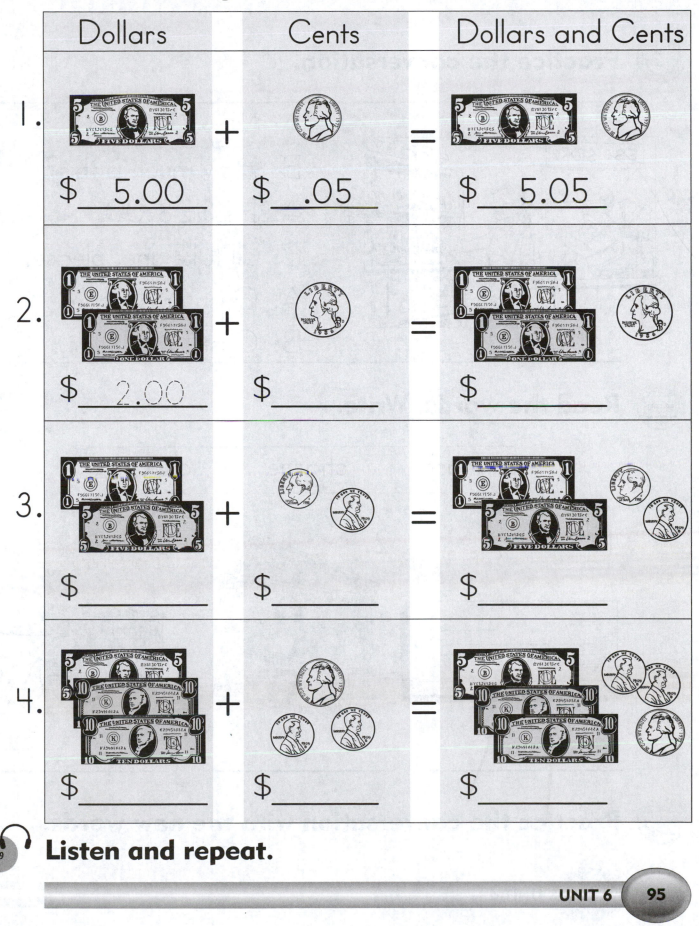		

1. $ __5.00__ + $ __.05__ = $ __5.05__

2. $ __2.00__ + $ _____ = $ _____

3. $ _____ + $ _____ = $ _____

4. $ _____ + $ _____ = $ _____

🎧 **Listen and repeat.**
49

Listen to the conversation.

Practice the conversation.

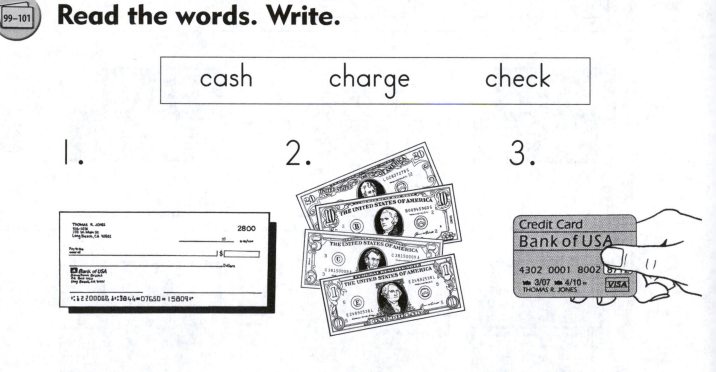

A: May I help you?

B: How much is this?

A: It's $28.00.

B: I'll take one, please.

A: <u>Cash</u> or <u>charge</u>?

B: <u>Cash</u>.

99–101 Read the words. Write.

cash	charge	check

1. _____

2. _____

3. _____

Practice the conversation with the new words.

Listen and circle.

1.	5¢	10¢	15¢
2.	25¢	50¢	75¢
3.	40¢	60¢	80¢
4.	55¢	65¢	95¢

5.	$10	$20	$30
6.	$11	$12	$13
7.	$15	$50	$55
8.	$78	$87	$88

9.	$12.50	$22.50	$32.50
10.	$28.10	$58.20	$88.30
11.	$9.50	$5.90	$9.05
12.	$17.85	$85.17	$70.80

Say the words. Write the numbers.

1	One		_____	Twenty-six
2	Two		_____	Twenty-seven
_____	Three		_____	Twenty-eight
_____	Four		29	Twenty-nine
_____	Five		_____	Thirty
_____	Six		_____	Thirty-one
_____	Seven		_____	Thirty-two
_____	Eight		33	Thirty-three
_____	Nine		_____	Thirty-four
10	Ten		_____	Thirty-five
_____	Eleven		36	Thirty-six
_____	Twelve		_____	Thirty-seven
13	Thirteen		_____	Thirty-eight
_____	Fourteen		_____	Thirty-nine
_____	Fifteen		_____	Forty
_____	Sixteen		_____	Forty-one
_____	Seventeen		42	Forty-two
_____	Eighteen		_____	Forty-three
19	Nineteen		_____	Forty-four
_____	Twenty		_____	Forty-five
_____	Twenty-one		_____	Forty-six
22	Twenty-two		_____	Forty-seven
_____	Twenty-three		_____	Forty-eight
_____	Twenty-four		_____	Forty-nine
_____	Twenty-five		50	Fifty

Read the check.

	March 8, 2007
PAY TO ___ABC Market___	$ __14.00__
__Fourteen and__ $^{no}/100$ ～ _____	DOLLARS
	___Mary Lee___

Write the check for $38.00.

	_____
PAY TO _____	$ _____
_____	DOLLARS
	_____

Write the check for $50.00.

	_____
PAY TO _____	$ _____
_____	DOLLARS
	_____

Say the words. Write the numbers.

_51_	Fifty-one	_____	Seventy-six
_____	Fifty-two	_____	Seventy-seven
_____	Fifty-three	_____	Seventy-eight
_____	Fifty-four	_____	Seventy-nine
_55_	Fifty-five	_80_	Eighty
_____	Fifty-six	_____	Eighty-one
_____	Fifty-seven	_____	Eighty-two
_58_	Fifty-eight	_83_	Eighty-three
_____	Fifty-nine	_____	Eighty-four
_____	Sixty	_____	Eighty-five
_61_	Sixty-one	_____	Eighty-six
_____	Sixty-two	_____	Eighty-seven
_____	Sixty-three	_____	Eighty-eight
_____	Sixty-four	_89_	Eighty-nine
_____	Sixty-five	_____	Ninety
_____	Sixty-six	_____	Ninety-one
_____	Sixty-seven	_92_	Ninety-two
_____	Sixty-eight	_____	Ninety-three
_69_	Sixty-nine	_____	Ninety-four
_____	Seventy	_____	Ninety-five
_____	Seventy-one	_____	Ninety-six
_72_	Seventy-two	_____	Ninety-seven
_____	Seventy-three	_____	Ninety-eight
_____	Seventy-four	_____	Ninety-nine
_____	Seventy-five	_100_	One hundred

Write the numbers for a check.

1. Sixty-one and 19/100   DOLLARS $ __61.19__

2. Thirty-four and no/100   DOLLARS $ __34.00__

3. Fifteen and 50/100   DOLLARS $ _____

4. One hundred and no/100 DOLLARS $ _____

5. Ninety-eight and 87/100 DOLLARS $ _____

6. Eleven and 25/100   DOLLARS $ _____

7. Forty and no/100   DOLLARS $ _____

Write the words for a check.

1. $10.00 | Ten and no/100 | DOLLARS

2. $10.10 | Ten and 10/100 | DOLLARS

3. $23.00 | | DOLLARS

4. $23.50 | | DOLLARS

5. $49.00 | | DOLLARS

6. $49.68 | | DOLLARS

7. $95.00 | | DOLLARS

Read the check.

March 8, 2007

PAY TO _ABC Market_ $ _87.50_

Eighty-seven and 50/100 ～ ———— **DOLLARS**

Mary Lee

Write the check for $61.99.

_____

PAY TO _____ $ _____

_____ **DOLLARS**

_____

Write the check for $90.18.

_____

PAY TO _____ $ _____

_____ **DOLLARS**

_____

Listen to the conversation.

Practice the conversation.

A: Do you have change?

B: Yes, I do.

A: Do you have <u>quarters</u>?

B: No, I don't.

A: Do you have <u>dimes</u>?

B: Yes, I do. I have <u>five dimes</u>.

Match.

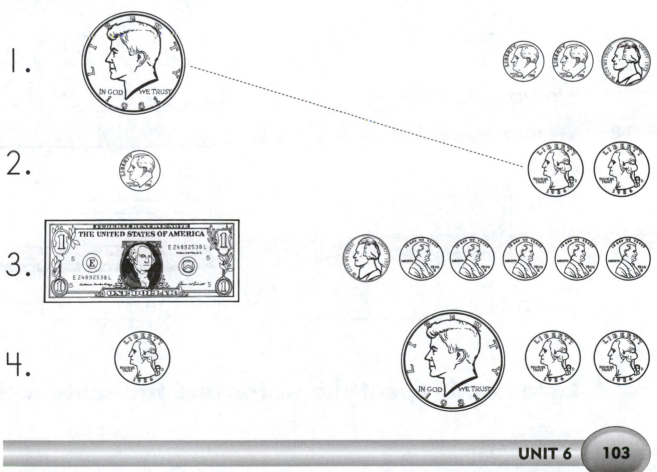

1.

2.

3.

4.

Write Ch **and** ch.

Ch ———————————————

ch ———————————————

Write ch **in the words. Read.**

___eck   ___ange   wat___

___arge   tea___er   lun___

Write the words in the sentences.

1.

Do you have _____?

2.

I eat _____ at 12:00.

3.

Cash or _____?

4.

Write the _____ for $20.

53 **Listen and repeat the words and the sentences.**

Listen to the conversation.

Practice the conversation.

EBC STORE

Television

Television · Tel

A: May I help you?

B: I want to buy this, please.

A: OK. It's $117.00.

B: Do you take checks?

A: Yes. I need your driver's license.

B: OK. Here you are.

Read the words. Write.

| ATM card | credit card | driver's license |
| green card | social security card | |

1. DMV CALIFORNIA
DRIVER LICENSE
N4174741   CLASS 3
EXPIRES ON   EXPIRES: 3-13-10
BIRTHDAY
THOMAS R. JONES
121 E 2ND ST
LONG BEACH CA 90802
SEX:M   HAIR:BLK EYES:BRN
HT:5-08 WT:170 DOB:03-13-58
RSTR: CORR LENS
X
6-19-05 507

_____

2. RESIDENT ALIEN
NGUYEN-DUC TRI

_____

3. SOCIAL   SECURITY
ACCOUNT   NUMBER
123-45-6789
HAS BEEN ESTABLISHED FOR
SIGNATURE
FOR SOCIAL SECURITY AND TAX PURPOSES—NOT FOR IDENTIFICATION

_____

4. Credit Card
State Bank
4305 0001 8003 8712
3/07   4/10
VISA
Jane Diaz

_____

5. 24-hour Banking
Bank of USA
434300 08 1000 5440
3/07   4/10 ex
SUSAN A. FUENTES

_____

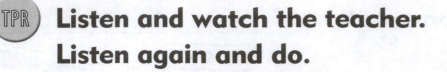

TPR **Listen and watch the teacher.**
Listen again and do.

- ◆ Take out your check.
- ◆ Write the check.
- ◆ Show your driver's license.
- ◆ Show your credit card.

Write the sentences.

1.

   _____

2.

   _____

3.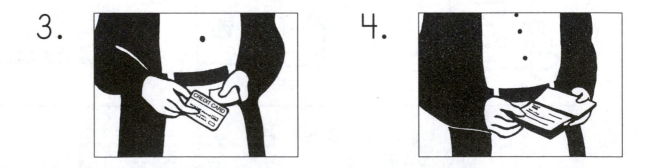

   _____

4.

   _____

Speak and write about how you pay the rent.

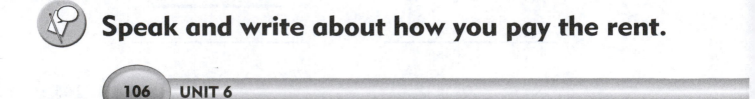

55
109-114

Listen to the story.
Listen again. Write the numbers 1 to 6.

 5

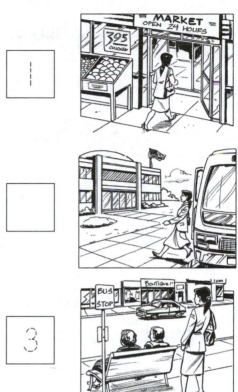 1

3

193 **Read the story.**

Write the story.

1. _____

2. _____

3. _____

4. _____

5. _____

6. _____

Answer the questions.
Write Yes, I do. **or** No, I don't.

1. Do you have change? _____

2. Do you have a driver's license? _____

3. Do you have a credit card? _____

4. Do you write checks? _____

5. Do you have an ATM card? _____

Ask your classmates.
Write yes **or** no.

Classmate's Name				
Change				
Driver's License				
ATM Card				
Credit Card				
Checks				

Write B and b.

B ‗ ‗ ‗ ‗ ‗ ‗ ‗

b ‗ ‗ ‗ ‗ ‗ ‗ ‗

Write b in the words. Read.

__us __ank __orn

__ook __uy __irthday

Listen. Write ch or b.

1. I wat___ TV at home.

2. Please write a ___eck.

3. I take the ___us to the ___ank.

4. The tea___er needs a ___air.

5. My ___irthday is in Septem___er.

Listen and repeat the words and the sentences.

Listen to the conversation.

Practice the conversation.

A: Hello. This is XYZ Radio. You won $500!
B: Really?
A: Yes. I just need your credit card number.
B: No, thanks. Goodbye.

Write the words.

Personal Information

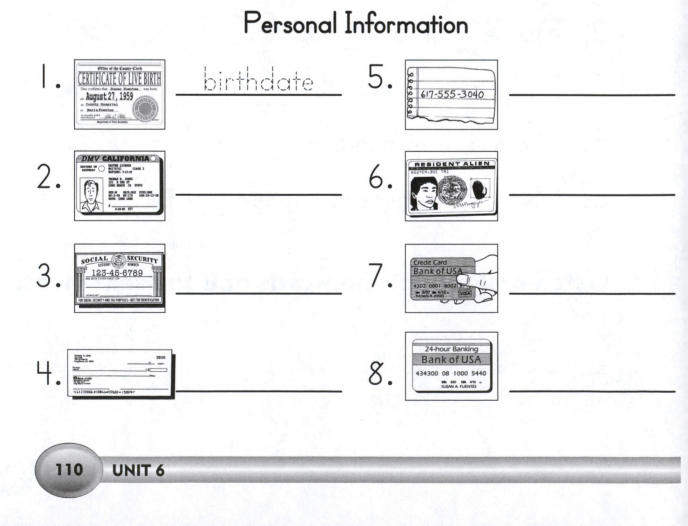

1. <u>birthdate</u>

2. _____

3. _____

4. _____

5. _____

6. _____

7. _____

8. _____

UNIT 6 REVIEW

Read.

1	one	11	eleven	21	twenty-one
2	two	12	twelve	30	thirty
3	three	13	thirteen	40	forty
4	four	14	fourteen	50	fifty
5	five	15	fifteen	60	sixty
6	six	16	sixteen	70	seventy
7	seven	17	seventeen	80	eighty
8	eight	18	eighteen	90	ninety
9	nine	19	nineteen	100	one hundred
10	ten	20	twenty	200	two hundred

Write a check for your telephone bill.

PAY TO _____ $ _____

_____ DOLLARS

Write a check for your rent.

PAY TO _____ $ _____

_____ DOLLARS

Ask your classmates.

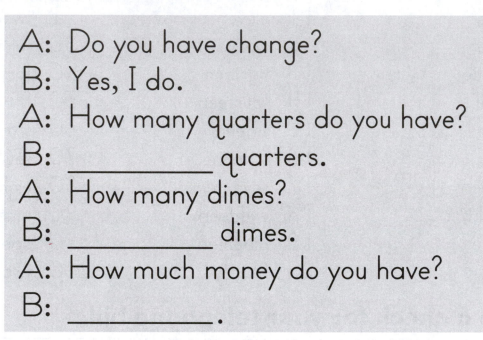

A: Do you have change?
B: Yes, I do.
A: How many quarters do you have?
B: _____ quarters.
A: How many dimes?
B: _____ dimes.
A: How much money do you have?
B: _____.

Write the number of quarters, dimes, nickels, and pennies.

Classmate's Name	Quarters	Dimes	Nickels	Pennies

Talk about your classmates.

Vin **has** 6 dimes and 2 quarters.
Fatima **has** 8 pennies, 3 nickels, and 4 dimes.

Write one amount of money in each box.

Write the $ and ¢ symbols in each square.

1¢	$ 1.00	$ 1.20	$ 1.80
10¢	$ 5.00	$ 12.00	$ 18.00
25¢	$ 10.00	$ 20.00	$ 80.00
50¢	$ 50.00	$ 120.00	$ 118.00

Listen. Write an X on the number your teacher says. The students with all Xs win.

Listen and point. Listen again and repeat.

1. husband   2. wife   3. mother   4. father

5. daughter   6. son   7. children   8. parents

Listen to the conversation.

Practice the conversation.

A: Who's he?

B: He's my son.

A: Who's she?

B: She's my daughter.

A: Who are they?

B: They're my father and mother.

Write He's, She's, **or** They're **in the sentences.**

1. _____She's_____ my mother.

2. _____ my husband.

3. _____ my son and daughter.

4. _____ my father.

5. _____ my wife.

6. _____ my daughter.

7. _____ my teacher.

8. _____ my son.

9. _____ my classmates.

10. _____ my children.

119 **Read. Circle** Yes **or** No.

1. I live with my mother.　Yes　No

2. I live with my father.　Yes　No

3. I have a wife.　Yes　No

4. I have a husband.　Yes　No

5. I have a son.　Yes　No

6. I have a daughter.　Yes　No

7. I have children.　Yes　No

Write the sentences with Yes **circled.**

_____

_____

_____

_____

_____

Bring family photos to class.
Ask about your classmates' photos.

Speak and write about your photos.

Listen to the conversation.

Practice the conversation.

A: This is my brother.
B: Nice to meet you.
C: Nice to meet you, too.

Read. Circle Yes **or** No.

1. I have one brother.   Yes   No

2. I have two brothers.   Yes   No

3. I have _____ brothers.   Yes   No
   number

4. I don't have any brothers.   Yes   No

5. I have one sister.   Yes   No

6. I have two sisters.   Yes   No

7. I have _____ sisters.   Yes   No
   number

8. I don't have any sisters.   Yes   No

Ask your classmates.

A: How many children do you have?

B: I have <u>two children, one daughter and one son.</u>

A: How many brothers and sisters do you have?

B: I have <u>one brother and two sisters.</u>

Write their answers.

Classmate's Name	Children	Sisters	Brothers

 Talk about your classmates.

Tina **doesn't have** any children.

She **has** one sister.

She **has** three brothers.

Write Th **and** th.

Th ___ ___ ___ ___ ___ ___
th ___ ___ ___ ___ ___ ___

Read. Circle the words with Th **or** th.

A: This is my mother and father.
B: Nice to meet you.
A: This is my brother.
B: Nice to meet you.

Write the words with Th **or** th.

1. _____
2. _____
3. _____
4. _____

Listen and repeat the conversation and the words.

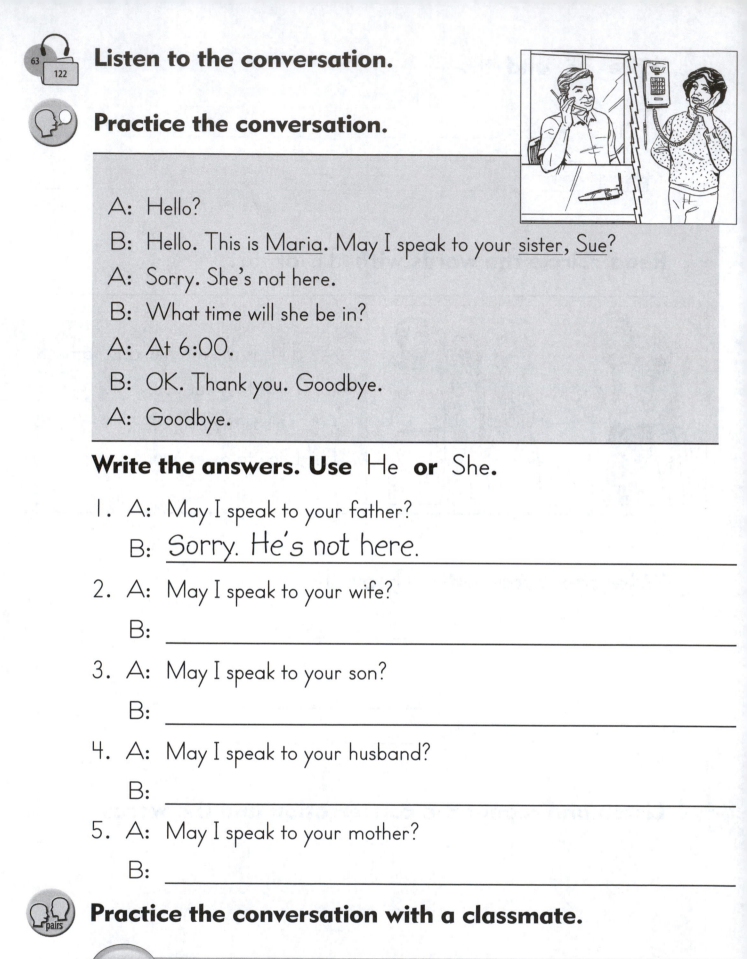

Listen to the conversation.

Practice the conversation.

A: Hello?

B: Hello. This is <u>Maria</u>. May I speak to your <u>sister</u>, <u>Sue</u>?

A: Sorry. She's not here.

B: What time will she be in?

A: At 6:00.

B: OK. Thank you. Goodbye.

A: Goodbye.

Write the answers. Use He **or** She**.**

1. A: May I speak to your father?

   B: <u>Sorry. He's not here.</u>

2. A: May I speak to your wife?

   B: _____

3. A: May I speak to your son?

   B: _____

4. A: May I speak to your husband?

   B: _____

5. A: May I speak to your mother?

   B: _____

Practice the conversation with a classmate.

Listen to the conversation.

Practice the conversation.

A: Hello?

B: Hello. This is <u>John</u>. May I speak to your <u>brother</u>, <u>Pete</u>?

A: Just a minute, please.

B: Thank you.

Write the answers.

1. A: May I speak to your mother?

   B: Just a minute, please.

2. A: May I speak to your daughter?

   B: Sorry, she's not here.

3. A: May I speak to your son?

   B: Just

4. A: May I speak to your father?

   B: Sorry

5. A: May I speak to your wife?

   B: Just

Practice the conversation with a classmate.

Write H and h.

H —————————————————————————————

h —————————————————————————————

Read. Circle the words beginning with H or h.

A: Hello?

B: Hi. This is Pedro. How are you?

A: I'm fine, thank you.

B: May I speak to your husband?

A: Sorry. He's not here.

B: When will he be in?

A: He'll be home at 6:30.

Write the words beginning with H or h.

1. _____   6. _____

2. _____   7. _____

3. _____   8. _____

4. _____   9. _____

5. _____

Listen and repeat the conversation and the words.

Listen and watch the teacher.

Listen again and do.

◆ Pick up the receiver.

◆ Dial the phone number.

◆ Talk on the phone.

◆ Hang up.

Write the sentences.

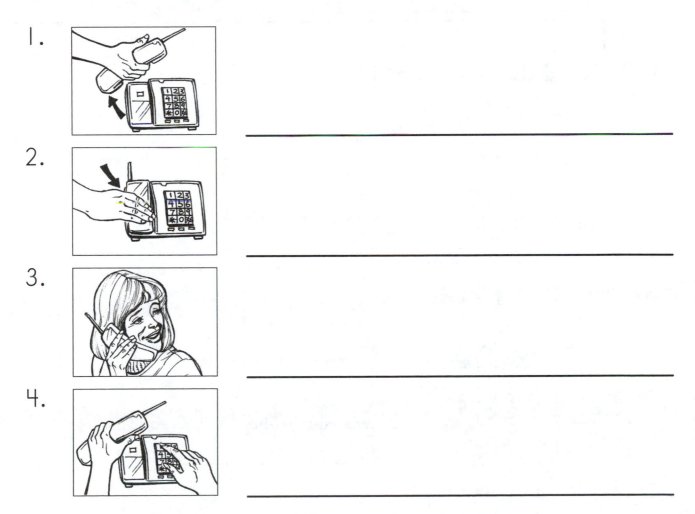

1. _____

2. _____

3. _____

4. _____

 Speak and write about how you use a phone.

Listen to the conversation.

Practice the conversation.

A: Hello. How are you?
B: Fine, thank you.
A: How's your sister, Sue?
B: She's <u>busy</u>.
   She has two jobs.

Read the words. Write.

sick	happy	tired	worried

1.
   How's your mother?
   She's _____.

2.
   How's your brother?
   He's _____.

3.
   How's your father?
   He's _____.

4.
   How's your daughter?
   She's _____.

130 **Match.**

tired

sick

busy

happy

worried

 Ask your classmates.

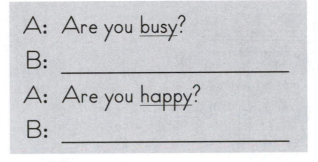

A: Are you <u>busy</u>?

B: _____

A: Are you <u>happy</u>?

B: _____

Write yes **or** no.

Classmate's Name	busy	happy	sick	tired	worried

Talk about your classmates.

Marco **is** worried.   Nina and Ali **are** happy.

Listen to the story.
Listen again. Write the numbers 1 to 6.

194

Read the story.

Write the story.

1. _____

2. _____

3. _____

4. _____

5. _____

6. _____

Complete your story. Tell your story to a classmate.

1. I'm _____.
   name

2. I'm from _____.
   birthplace

3. I'm _____ years old.
   age

4. I _____ every day.

5. I'm a good _____.

6. I'm very _____.

 Ask a classmate. Write your classmate's story.

1. This is _____.
   name

2. _____'s from _____.
   birthplace

3. _____'s _____ years old.
   age

4. _____ _____ every day.

5. _____'s a good _____.

6. _____'s very _____.

Talk about your classmate.

137 **Fill out the form.**

_____	_____	_____
First Name	Middle Name	Last Name

Address _____

City   State   Zip Code

Telephone _____   Sex ☐ F
                                                    ☐ M   Age _____

═══════════════════════════════════════

Husband/Wife's Name _____

Children's Names   Ages

_____   _____

_____   _____

_____   _____

═══════════════════════════════════════

Father's Name _____

Mother's Name _____

Number of Brothers _____

Number of Sisters _____

Match.

1. Who's he?   I don't have any children.

2. How many sisters do you have?   He's my father.

3. How many children do you have?   I have two sisters.

---

4. This is my brother.   Sorry. She's not here.

5. May I speak to your mother?   Nice to meet you.

6. May I speak to your son?   Just a minute, please.

---

7. How are you?   Fine, thank you.

8. How's your husband?   Hello.

9. Hello.   He's busy.

---

10. Are you sick?   No, I'm tired.

11. Who are they?   At 3:00.

12. What time will your sister,   They're my children.
    Sue, be in?

UNIT 7 REVIEW

Write a word in each box.

wife	children	mother	brothers	sisters
sons	sister	husband	daughters	parents
father	daughter	son	brother	family

**Listen. Write an ✕ on the word your teacher says.
The students with all ✕s win.**

68 **138** **Listen and point. Listen again and repeat.**

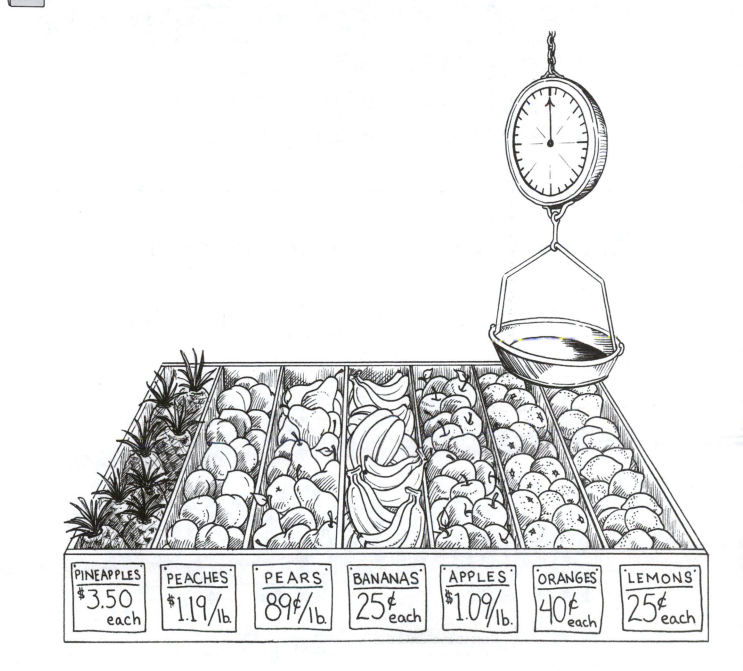

PINEAPPLES $3.50 each

PEACHES $1.19/lb.

PEARS 89¢/lb.

BANANAS 25¢ each

APPLES $1.09/lb.

ORANGES 40¢ each

LEMONS 25¢ each

69 **139** **Listen to the conversation.**

Practice the conversation.

> A: May I help you?
>
> B: What's in the fruit salad?
>
> A: <u>Oranges</u>, <u>pears</u>, <u>apples</u>, and <u>bananas</u>.
>
> B: OK. I want the fruit salad, please.

 140-146 **Write the word for two or more (the plural).**

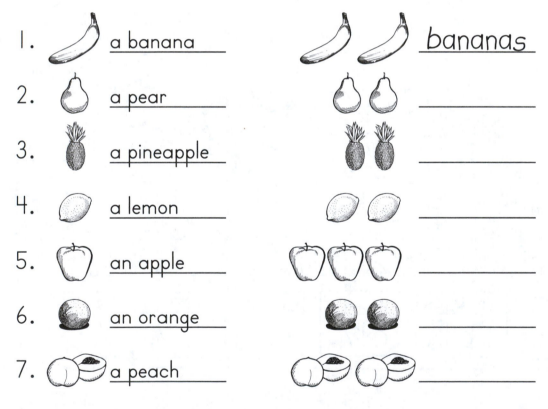

1. a banana   _bananas_

2. a pear   _____

3. a pineapple   _____

4. a lemon   _____

5. an apple   _____

6. an orange   _____

7. a peach   _____

Practice the conversation with the new words.

Ask your classmates.

A: What fruits do you like?	A: Do you like <u>bananas</u>?
B: I like _____.	B: _____.

Write the answers.

Classmate's Name	Likes	Doesn't Like

Write sentences about your classmates.

1. _____ likes _____.
        Name

   _____ doesn't like _____.
        He/She

2. _____ likes _____.

   _____ doesn't like _____.

3. _____ _____ _____.

   _____ _____ _____.

Listen to the conversation.

Practice the conversation.

> A: I want to buy <u>two apples</u>, please.
>
> B: OK. That's <u>$1.50</u>.
>
> A: And <u>three bananas</u>.
>
> B: That's <u>$2.10</u> in all.

Look at the fruit stand. Write the answers.

1. How much is an orange? <u> $1.00 </u>

2. How much is an apple? _____

3. How much is a pear? _____

4. How much are two bananas? _____

5. How much are a pear and an orange? _____

6. How much are two apples and a banana? _____

Listen and watch the teacher.

Listen again and do.

- Wash the apple.
- Peel the apple.
- Slice the apple.
- Eat the apple.

Write the sentences.

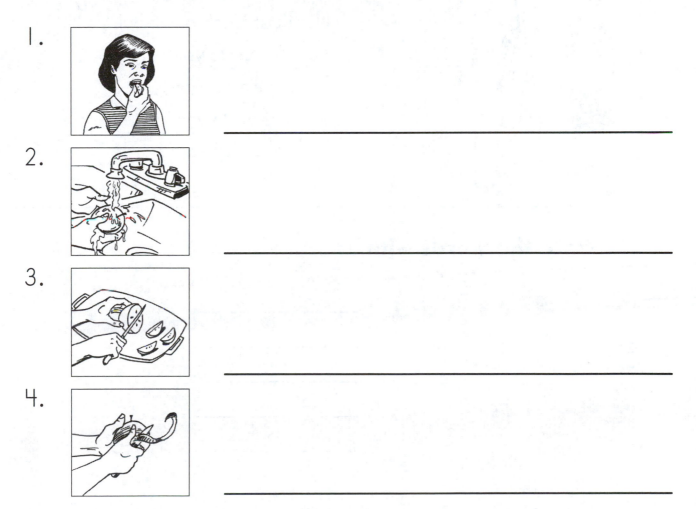

1.

2.

3.

4.

Speak and write about how you make a fruit salad.

Write L and l.

57 Read. Circle the words with l.

A: Where do you eat lunch?

B: I eat lunch at school.

A: When do you eat?

B: At eleven–thirty.

A: What do you eat?

B: I like fruit salad.

Write the words with l.

1. _____

2. _____

3. _____

4. _____

5. _____

71 Listen and repeat the conversation and the words.

Listen to the conversation.

Practice the conversation.

A: May I help you?

B: I want a hamburger.

A: With lettuce, tomatoes, and onions?

B: I want lettuce and tomatoes, but no onions.

A: Anything else?

B: No, thanks.

Read and circle.

1. (carrot) potato	2. pepper onion	3. potato mushroom	4. potato tomato
5. fruit pepper	6. mushroom carrot	7. lettuce tomato	8. fruits vegetables

149-153 **Write the word for two or more (the plural).**

1. a pepper   peppers

2. a carrot

3. an onion

4. a potato

5. a tomato

 Ask your classmates.

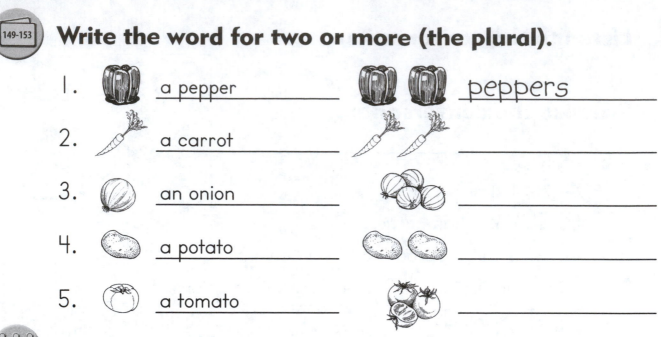

A: What vegetables do you like?

B: I like _____.

A: Do you like <u>mushrooms</u>?

B: _____

Write the answers.

Classmate's Name	Likes	Doesn't Like

Talk about your classmates.

Maria **likes** onions.   Ping **doesn't like** peppers.

Look at the fruits and vegetables.

Answer the questions.

1. How much are onions? _____ 79¢ a pound _____

2. How much are mushrooms? _____

3. How much is a pineapple? _____

4. How much are carrots? _____

Write is or are.

1. How much ___ is ___ a pineapple?

2. How much ___ are ___ potatoes?

3. How much _____ a banana?

4. How much _____ apples?

5. How much _____ tomatoes?

6. How much _____ a lemon?

7. How much _____ carrots and onions?

8. How much _____ two bananas?

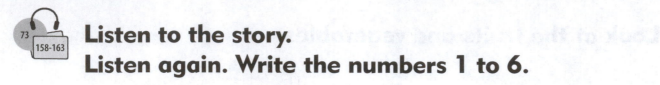

73 **158-163** **Listen to the story.**
Listen again. Write the numbers 1 to 6.

☐	☐
1	☐
☐	4

195 **Read the story.**

Write the story.

1. _____

2. _____

3. _____

4. _____

5. _____

6. _____

Check (✓) what you like for breakfast.

- ☐ soup
- ☐ eggs
- ☐ fruit
- ☐ donut
- ☐ cereal
- ☐ _____

Check (✓) what you like for lunch.

- ☐ noodles
- ☐ hamburger
- ☐ sandwich
- ☐ salad
- ☐ pizza
- ☐ _____

Check (✓) what you like for dinner.

- ☐ rice
- ☐ vegetables
- ☐ fish
- ☐ steak
- ☐ chicken
- ☐ _____

Check (✓) what you like to drink.

- ☐ tea
- ☐ coffee
- ☐ milk
- ☐ soda
- ☐ juice
- ☐ _____

Ask your classmates.

A: What do you like to eat?

B: I like _____.

A: What do you like to drink?

B: _____

Write the food and drinks.

Classmate's Name	Food	Drinks

Write sentences like this.

1. _____ likes to eat _____ and drink _____.
   Name

2. _____

3. _____

4. _____

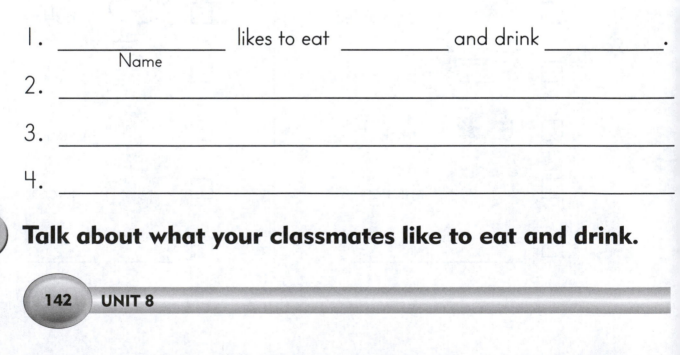 **Talk about what your classmates like to eat and drink.**

Write Sh **and** sh.

Sh

sh

Write sh **in the words. Read.**

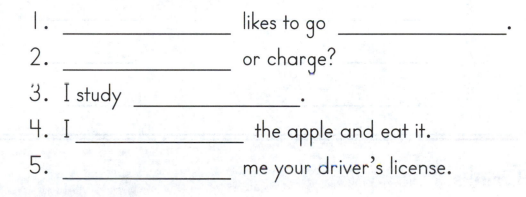

____e   wa____   ____ow

____opping   ca____   Engli____

Listen. Write the words.
Listen again and repeat.

1. _____ likes to go _____.

2. _____ or charge?

3. I study _____.

4. I _____ the apple and eat it.

5. _____ me your driver's license.

Listen. Write sh **or** ch **in the words.**
Listen again and repeat.

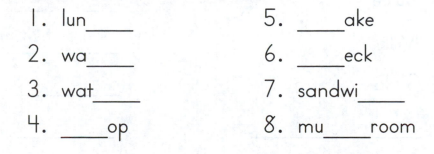

1. lun____   5. ____ake

2. wa____   6. ____eck

3. wat____   7. sandwi____

4. ____op   8. mu____room

Go to the cafeteria, restaurant, or coffee truck. Look at the menu. Write the price.

Foods

1. Hamburger $ _____
2. Salad   _____
3. Chicken   _____
4. Sandwich   _____
5. Donut   _____
6. _____   _____
7. _____   _____
8. _____   _____

Drinks

9. Coffee $ _____
10. Tea   _____
11. Juice   _____
12. Milk   _____
13. Soda   _____
14. _____   _____

Match.

1. Do you like pineapples?   Oranges, apples, and bananas.

2. How much is a pear?   It's 35¢.

3. What's in the fruit salad?   Yes, I do.

---

4. May I help you?   I want a hamburger.

5. What vegetables do you like?   Yes, please. I do.

6. Do you want onions?   I like potatoes.

---

7. What do you like to drink?   I like chicken.

8. Anything else?   No, thanks.

9. What do you like to eat?   I like coffee.

---

10. How much are the tomatoes?   He likes peaches and pears.

11. When do you eat lunch?   99¢ a pound.

12. What fruits does he like?   At 12:30.

UNIT 8 REVIEW

Write the words under fruits, vegetables, drinks, or food.

Fruits	Vegetables	Drinks	Food
			chicken

apple	lemon	potato
banana	lettuce	rice
carrot	milk	sandwich
✓chicken	noodles	soda
coffee	onion	soup
fish	orange	tea
hamburger	peach	tomato
juice	pizza	

76 164

Listen and point. Listen again and repeat.

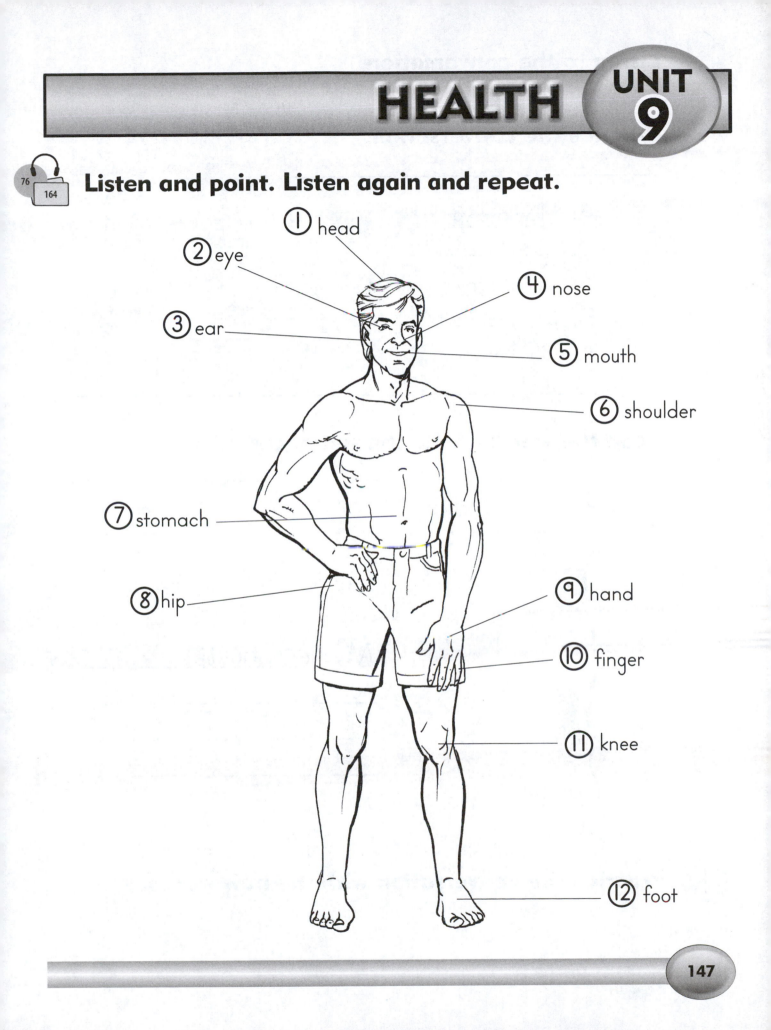

1 head
2 eye
3 ear
4 nose
5 mouth
6 shoulder
7 stomach
8 hip
9 hand
10 finger
11 knee
12 foot

Listen to the conversation.

Practice the conversation.

A: How are you?

B: I don't feel well.

A: What's the matter?

B: <u>My back hurts.</u>

A: Oh, I'm sorry.

Read the words. Write the sentences.

neck	chest	arm	leg

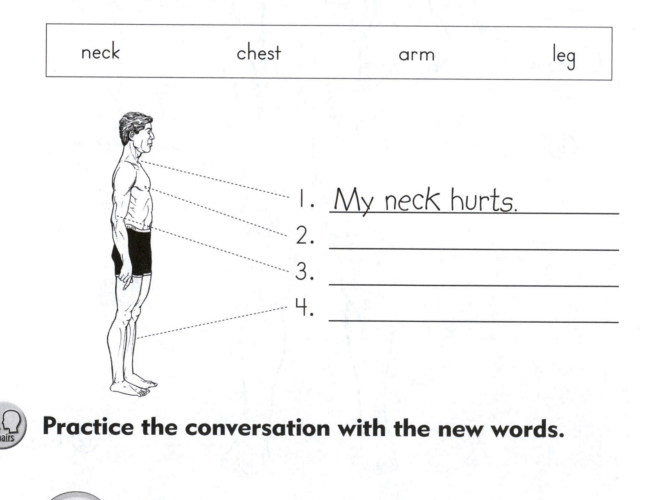

1. <u>My neck hurts.</u>

2. _____

3. _____

4. _____

Practice the conversation with the new words.

Listen to the conversation.

Practice the conversation.

A: Hello. Doctor's office.
B: I need to see the doctor.
A: What's the matter?
B: I have <u>a fever</u>.
A: Can you come at 3:00 today?
B: Yes, I can.

167-170 Read the words. Write the sentences.

| a cough | a headache | a cold | the flu |

1.

I have the flu.

2.

3.

4.

Practice the conversation with the new words.

Write M **and** m.

M ———————————— ————————————

m ———————————— ————————————

Read. Circle the words with M **or** m.

A: May I help you?
B: I need to see the doctor.
A: What's the matter?
B: My arm hurts.

Write the words with M **or** m.

1. _____   3. _____
2. _____   4. _____

Listen and repeat the conversation and the words.

Listen. Write m **or** n **in the words.**
Listen again and repeat.

1. ___onth   4. ___outh
2. ___ose   5. k___ee
3. ___eed   6. ___oney

172-174 **Write** doctor, dentist, **or** eye doctor.

 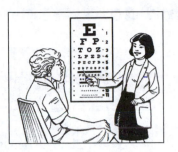 

_____   _____   _____

Ask your classmates.

A: Do you get checkups? Do you go to a doctor?

B: _____

A: Do you go to a dentist?

B: _____

A: Do you go to an eye doctor?

B: _____

Write yes **or** no.

Classmate's Name	Doctor	Dentist	Eye Doctor

Talk about your classmates.

Ann **goes** to a doctor. She **doesn't go** to a dentist or an eye doctor.

Listen and watch the teacher.

Listen again and do.

- ◆ Sit on the table.
- ◆ Open your mouth. Say ahh.
- ◆ Breathe in. Breathe out.
- ◆ Lie down.

Write the sentences.

1.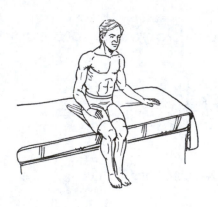

_____

_____

2.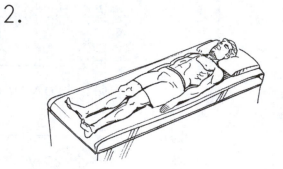

_____

_____

3.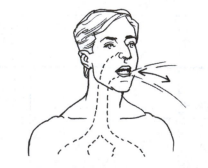

_____

_____

4.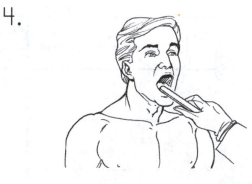

_____

_____

Speak and write about what you do at the doctor's office.

Write to your child's teacher.

_____
Date

Dear _____,
Teacher's Name

Please excuse my son _____.
Son's Name

He was absent yesterday because he had a cold.

Sincerely,

_____
Mother or Father's Name

_____
Date

Dear _____,
Teacher's Name

Please excuse my daughter _____.
Daughter's Name

She was absent yesterday because she had a fever.

Sincerely,

_____
Mother or Father's Name

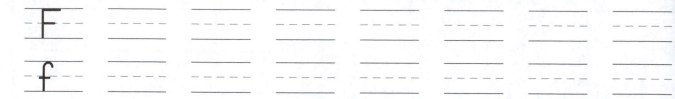

Write F and f.

F

f

Read. Circle the words with F or f.

A: How are you?
B: Fine, thank you.
A: How's your family?
B: My father's sick.
A: What's the matter?
B: He has the flu.

Write the words with F or f.

1. _____   3. _____

2. _____   4. _____

Listen and repeat the conversation and the words.

**Listen. Write f or v in the words.
Listen again and repeat.**

1. ___ever   4. co___ ___ee

2. ___ery   5. ___oot

3. ___egetable   6. ha___e

Listen to the story.

Listen again. Write the numbers 1 to 6.

Read the story.

Write the story.

1. _____

2. _____

3. _____

4. _____

5. _____

6. _____

Ask your classmates.

A: Do you exercise?

B: _____

A: Do you smoke?

B: _____

A: Do you have any problems?

B: <u>Sometimes my back hurts.</u>

Write the answers.

Classmate's Name	Exercise	Smoke	Problems

 Ask your class the questions. Write the answers.

1. How many students exercise? _____

2. How many students smoke? _____

3. How many students eat fruits? _____

4. How many students eat vegetables? _____

5. How many students get checkups? _____

6. How many students sleep seven hours? _____

Listen and point. Listen again and repeat.

85 **182** **Listen to the conversation.**

Practice the conversation.

> A: 911. What's your emergency?
> B: Help! My friend needs an ambulance.
> A: What's the matter?
> B: <u>He can't breathe.</u>
> A: Where are you?
> B: The address is _____.

183-186 **Read and write the sentences.**

She can't get up.	He's unconscious.
He's bleeding.	His chest hurts.

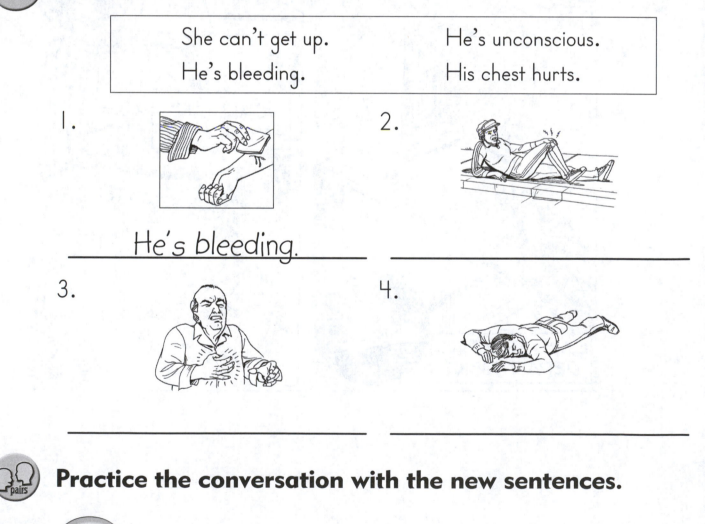

1.

_____He's bleeding._____

2.

_____

3.

_____

4.

_____

Practice the conversation with the new sentences.

Listen to the conversation.

Practice the conversation.

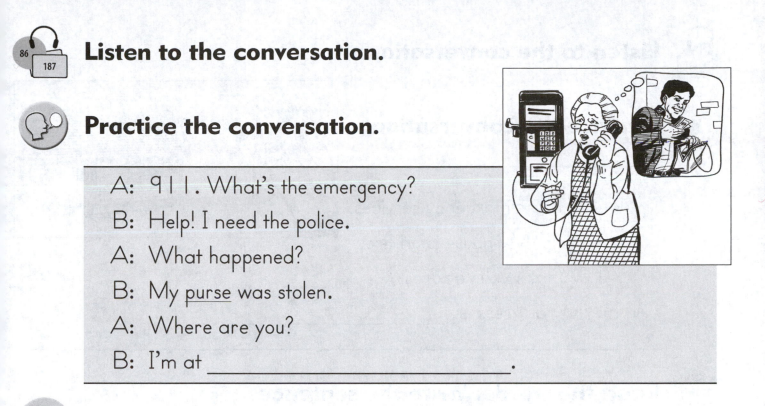

A: 911. What's the emergency?

B: Help! I need the police.

A: What happened?

B: My <u>purse</u> was stolen.

A: Where are you?

B: I'm at _____.

188-191 **Read the words. Write the sentences.**

| wallet | watch | car | bicycle |

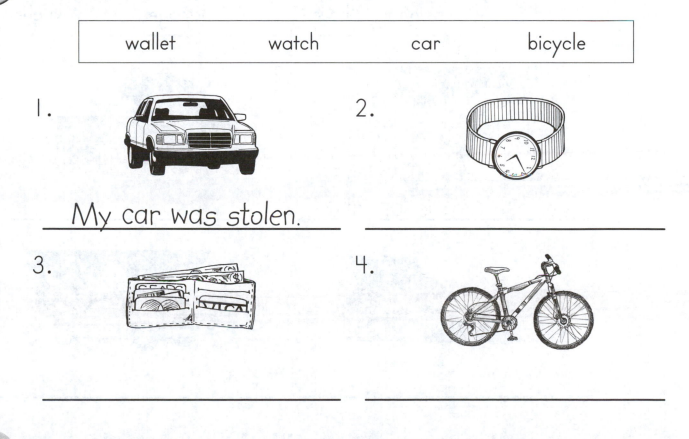

1.

My car was stolen.

2.

3.

4.

Practice the conversation with the new words.

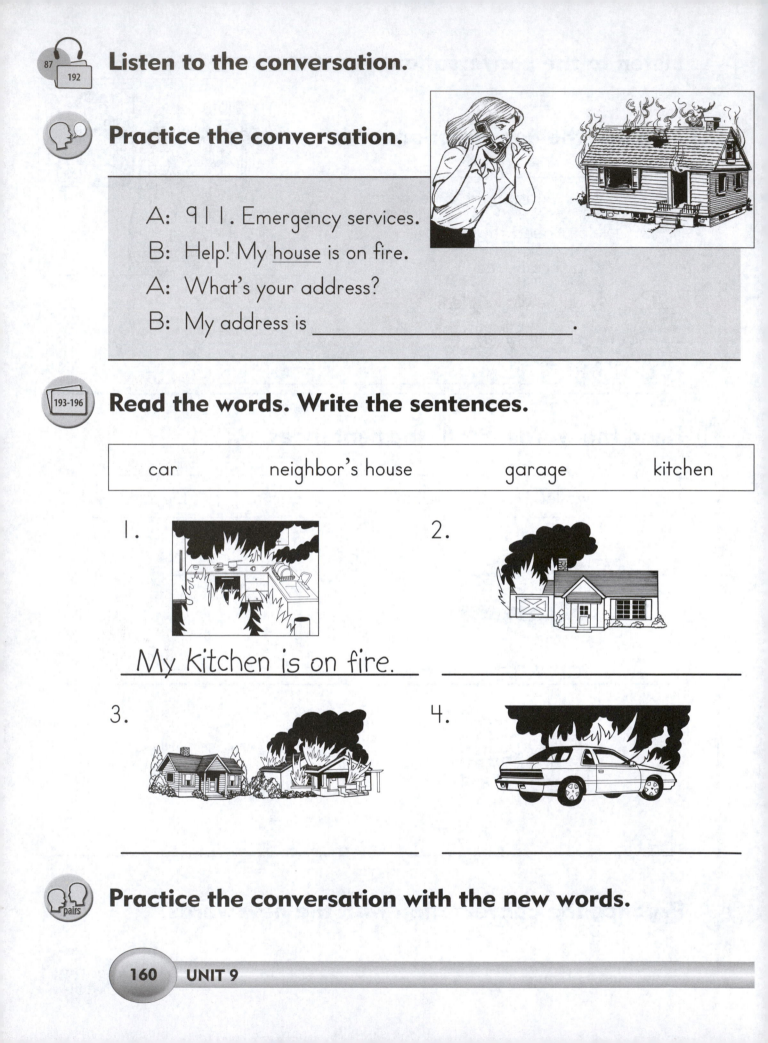

Listen to the conversation.

87 | 192

Practice the conversation.

A: 911. Emergency services.

B: Help! My <u>house</u> is on fire.

A: What's your address?

B: My address is _____.

193-196

Read the words. Write the sentences.

| car | neighbor's house | garage | kitchen |

1.

My kitchen is on fire.   _____

2.

_____

3.

_____

4.

_____

Practice the conversation with the new words.

Match.

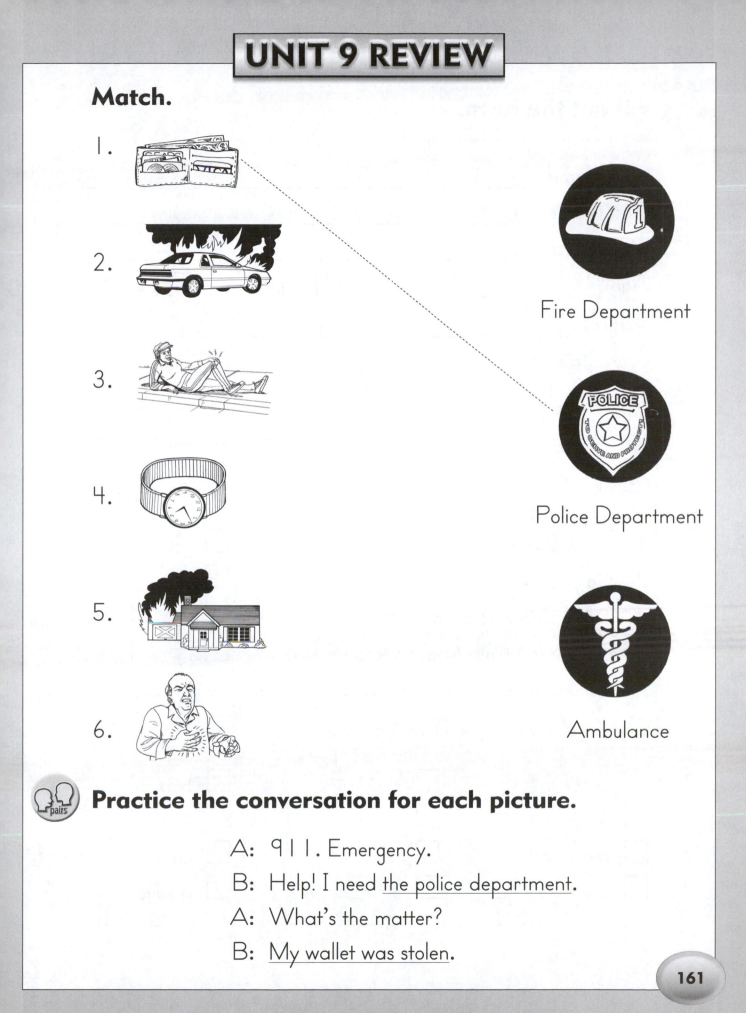

Fire Department

Police Department

Ambulance

Practice the conversation for each picture.

A: 911. Emergency.

B: Help! I need <u>the police department</u>.

A: What's the matter?

B: <u>My wallet was stolen</u>.

197 **Fill out the form.**

Last Name _____

First Name _____

Middle Name _____

Age _____ ☐ Male ☐ Female

Address _____

City, State, Zip Code _____

Telephone Number (_____) _____

Check (✔) Yes or No.

	Yes	No
1. Do you smoke?	☐	☐
2. Do you exercise?	☐	☐
3. Do you sleep seven hours?	☐	☐
4. Do you eat fruits/vegetables?	☐	☐

Check (✔) where you have problems.

☐ eyes	☐ shoulders	☐ hips
☐ ears	☐ chest	☐ legs
☐ neck	☐ arms	☐ knees
☐ back	☐ stomach	☐ ankles

Match.

1. How are you?   My back hurts.

2. What's the matter?   Yes, I do.

3. Do you get checkups?   I don't feel well.

---

4. 911. Emergency.   My money was stolen.

5. What happened?   My address is _____.

6. What's your address?   Help! I need the police.

---

7. What's the matter?   My chest hurts.

8. Do you smoke?   Yes. I walk to school.

9. Do you exercise?   No, I don't.

---

10. My leg hurts.   My mother's sick.

11. Can I see the doctor at 3:00? Oh. I'm sorry.

12. How's your family?   Yes, you can.

Write one word in each box.

stomach	hand	eye	leg	head
back	ankle	shoulder	arm	ear
chest	mouth	neck	knee	foot

**Listen. Write an ✕ on the word your teacher says.
The students with all ✕s win.**

88
198-203

Listen and point. Listen again and repeat.

1.

a factory worker

2.

a restaurant worker

3.

a sales clerk

4.

an office worker

5.

a hospital worker

6.

a garment worker

Listen to the conversation.

89 204

Practice the conversation.

A: Do you have a job?

B: Yes, I do.

A: What do you do?

B: I'm a <u>sales clerk</u>.

205-208 **Read the words. Write the sentences.**

bus driver	mechanic	security guard	teacher's aide

1.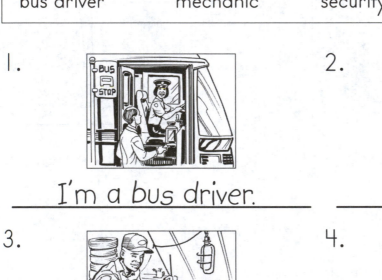

I'm a bus driver.

2.

_____

3.

4.

_____   _____

Practice the conversation with the new words.

Ask your classmates.

A: Do you want to be a <u>sales clerk</u>?

B: _____

A: Do you want to be a <u>mechanic</u>?

B: _____

Write yes, no, or maybe.

Job	Classmate 1	Classmate 2	Classmate 3
restaurant worker			
garment worker			
hospital worker			
factory worker			
office worker			
sales clerk			
mechanic			
teacher's aide			
bus driver			
security guard			

Speak and write about your classmates.

Lisa **wants** to be a bus driver.

Tina **doesn't want** to be a security guard.

Write J and j.

J ___ ___ ___ ___ ___ ___

j ___ ___ ___ ___ ___ ___

Write J and j in the words. Read.

___anuary   ___une   ___ust

___ob   ___uice   ___uly

Write the words in the sentences.

1. I drink _____.

2. The first month is _____.

3. _____ a minute, please.

Write J , j, or y in the words. Read.

1. ___ob   3. ___es   5. ___our   7. ___uly

2. ___ou   4. ___une   6. ___uice   8. ___ear

Listen and repeat the sentences and the words.

TPR **Listen and watch the teacher.**
Listen again and do.

- Take the box to the table.
- Put the box down.
- Pick the box up.
- Give the box to the customer.

Write the sentences.

1.

_____

_____

2.

_____

_____

3.

_____

_____

4.

_____

_____

Speak and write about what you do at work.

Write the capital letters.

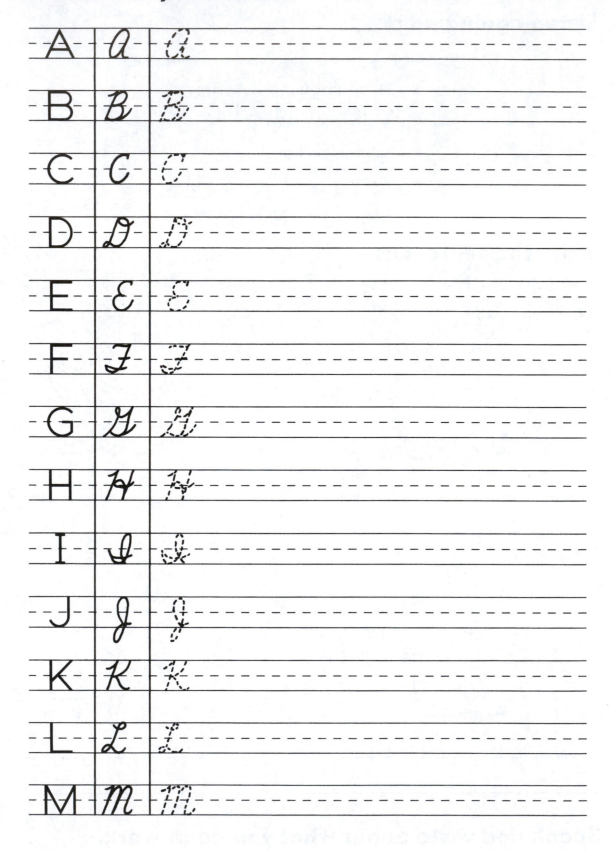

A   𝒜   𝒜

B   ℬ   ℬ

C   𝒞   𝒞

D   𝒟   𝒟

E   ℰ   ℰ

F   ℱ   ℱ

G   𝒢   𝒢

H   ℋ   ℋ

I   ℐ   ℐ

J   𝒥   𝒥

K   𝒦   𝒦

L   ℒ   ℒ

M   ℳ   ℳ

Write the capital letters.

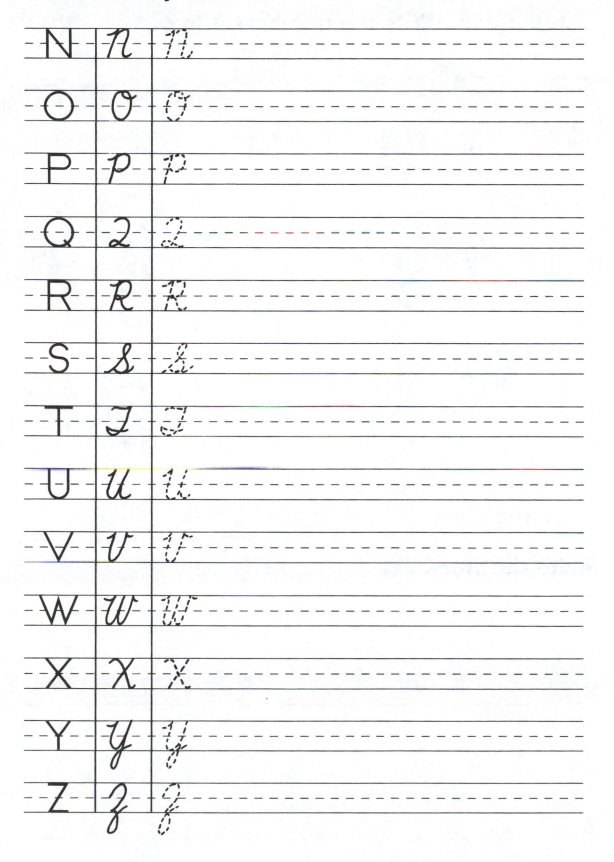

91 | 209-214

Listen to the story.
Listen again. Write the numbers 1 to 6.

[1]

[ ]

[ ]

[ ]

[2]

[ ]

197 **Read the story.**

Write the story.

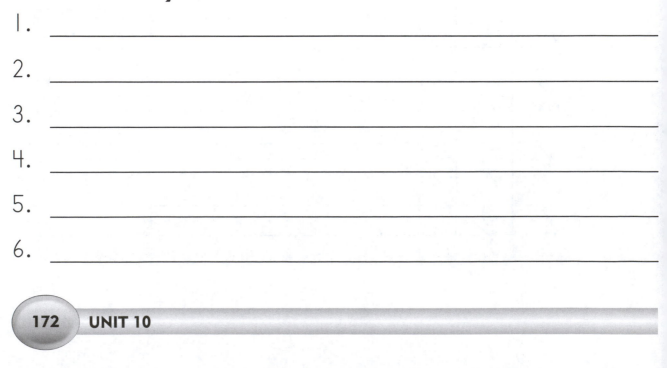

1. _____
2. _____
3. _____
4. _____
5. _____
6. _____

Write R and r.

R — — — — — — —

r — — — — — — —

Write r in the words. Read.

___est___oom   custome___   teache___

___estau___ant   fi___e   wo___ke___

Write the words in the sentences.

1. MEN WOMEN   Excuse me. Where's the _____?

2.   I'm a _____ worker.

3.   Help! My house is on _____.

Write r or l in the words. Read.

1. ___ead   3. worke___   5. schoo___   7. d___ink

2. ___ook   4. ___ike   6. w___ite   8. ___ong

 **Listen and repeat the sentences and the words.**

92

Read the time card.

	In	Lunch Out	Lunch In	Out	Total Hours
				TG AUTO	

TG AUTO

Employee <u>John Lee</u> Date <u>April 1-7</u>

	In	Lunch Out	Lunch In	Out	Total Hours
Sun.					
Mon.	8:00	12:00	1:00	5:00	8
Tues.	8:00	12:00	1:00	5:00	8
Wed.	8:00	12:00	1:00	5:00	8
Thurs.	8:00	12:00	1:00	5:00	8
Fri.	8:00	12:00	1:00	5:00	8
Sat.					
				Total Hours for Week	40

Write Yes, he does, No, he doesn't, **or** I don't know.

1. Does John work on Friday? _____.

2. Does he go to work at 12:00? _____.

3. Does he go to school at 6:00? _____.

4. Does he eat lunch at home? _____.

5. Does he work 5 days a week? _____.

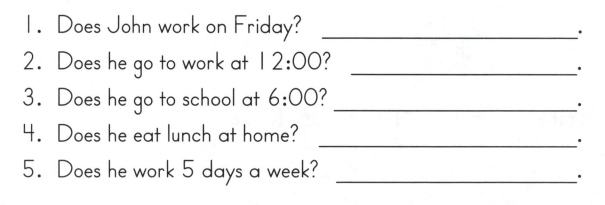

Speak and write about John Lee.

216 **Fill out your time card.**

	In	Lunch Out	Lunch In	Out	Total Hours
Company _____
Employee _____ Date _____
Sun.					
Mon.					
Tues.					
Wed.					
Thurs.					
Fri.					
Sat.					
				Total Hours for Week	

Ask a classmate.

1. Do you work Monday to Friday? _____

2. What time do you go to work? _____

3. What time do you eat lunch? _____

4. What time do you go home? _____

5. How many hours do you work in one day? _____

6. How many hours do you work in one week? _____

Speak and write about your classmate.

Write the small letters.

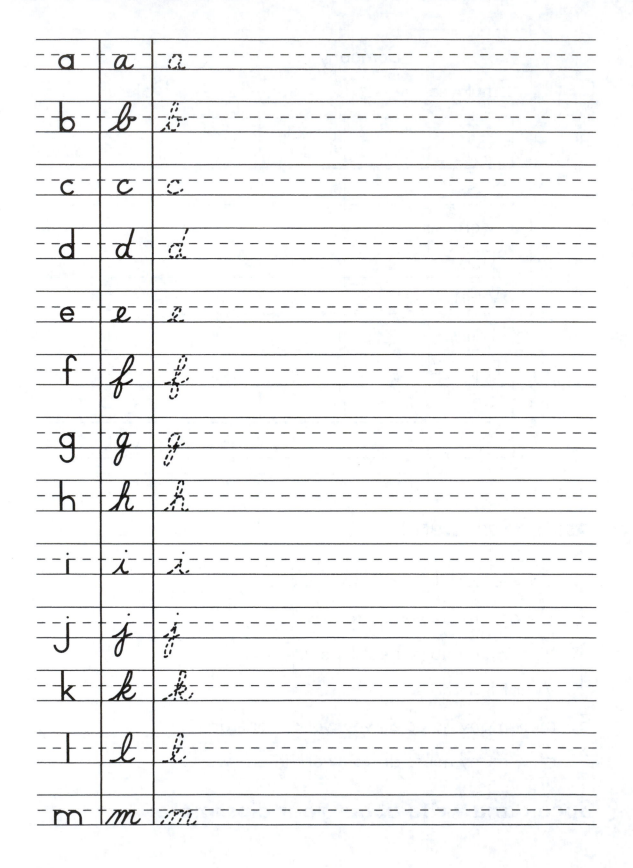

Write the small letters.

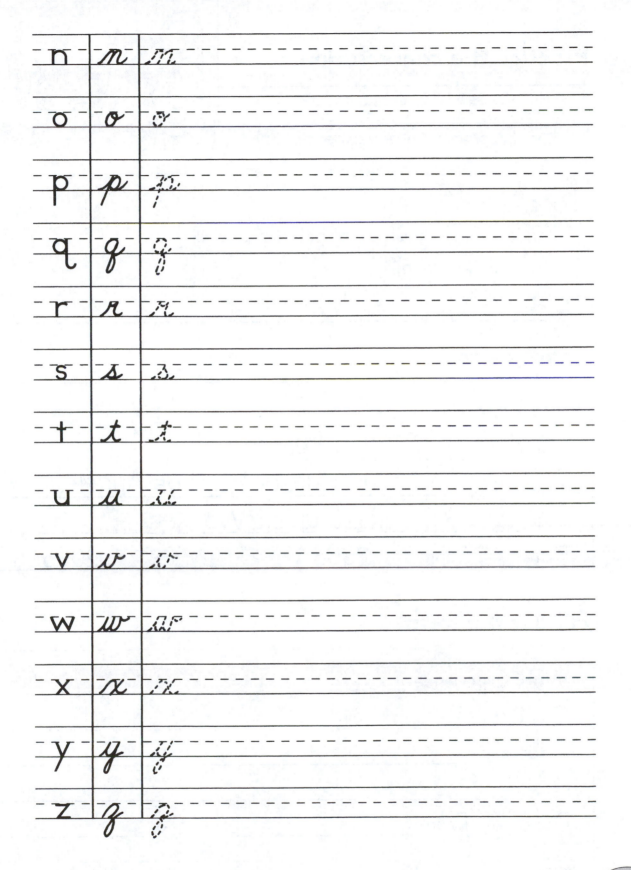

Listen to the conversation.

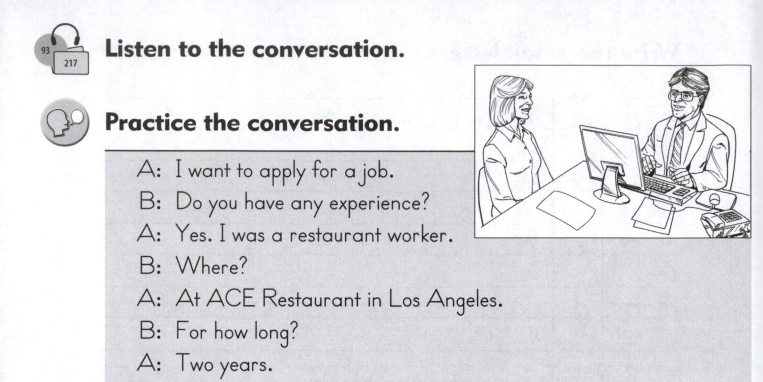

Practice the conversation.

A: I want to apply for a job.

B: Do you have any experience?

A: Yes. I was a restaurant worker.

B: Where?

A: At ACE Restaurant in Los Angeles.

B: For how long?

A: Two years.

Read the form.

Work Experience

Company ___ ACE Restaurant ___

Address ___ 100 Sunset St., Los Angeles ___

Job ___ Restaurant Worker ___

Date: From ___ 2003 ___   To ___ 2005 ___

Fill out the form.

Work Experience

Company ___

Address ___

Job ___

Date: From ___   To ___

Ask your classmates.

A: Do you have work experience?

B: Yes. I was a _____.

A: Where?

B: _____

A: For how long?

B: _____

Write their answers.

Classmate's Name	Experience	Where	How Long

Write sentences like this.

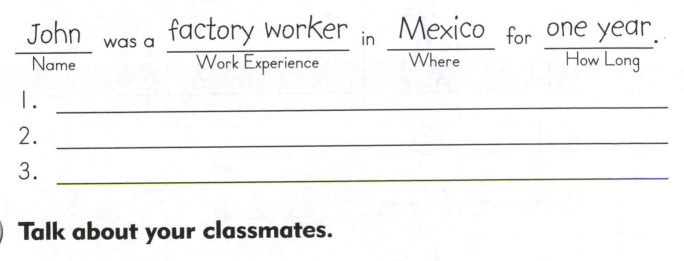

John was a factory worker in Mexico for one year.
Name — Work Experience — Where — How Long

1. _____

2. _____

3. _____

Talk about your classmates.

Write the capital and small letters.

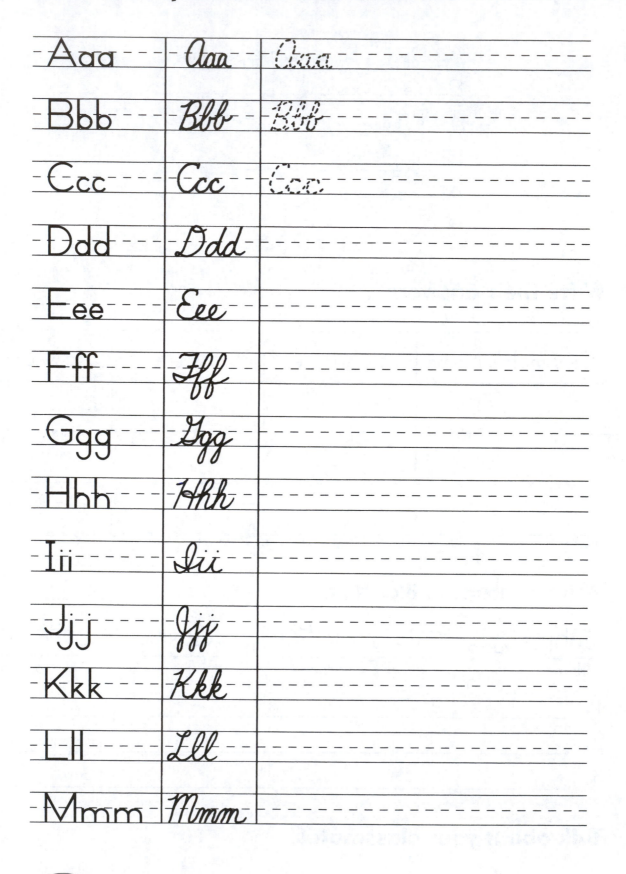

Aaa	Aaa	Aaa
Bbb	Bbb	Bbb
Ccc	Ccc	Ccc
Ddd	Ddd	
Eee	Eee	
Fff	Fff	
Ggg	Ggg	
Hhh	Hhh	
Iii	Iii	
Jjj	Jjj	
Kkk	Kkk	
Lll	Lll	
Mmm	Mmm	

Write the capital and small letters.

Nnn	Nnn
Ooo	Ooo
Ppp	Ppp
Qqq	Qqq
Rrr	Rrr
Sss	Sss
Ttt	Ttt
Uuu	Uuu
Vvv	Vvv
Www	Www
Xxx	Xxx
Yyy	Yyy
Zzz	Zzz

94 **218** **Listen to the conversation.**

 **Practice the conversation.**

A: May I help you?

B: I want to apply for a job.

A: Please fill out the application.

B: OK.

A: Please sign your name here.

B: OK. Thank you.

Practice your signature.

_____

- - - - - - - - - - - - - - - - - - -

_____

- - - - - - - - - - - - - - - - - - -

_____

- - - - - - - - - - - - - - - - - - -

Read and write.

Print your name. _____

                             First   Last

Signature _____

219 **Fill out the application.**

Date _____

Name _____ _____ _____
         Last   First   Middle

Address _____
                                    Street

_____ _____ _____
         City   State   Zip Code

Telephone (_____) _____

Position desired _____

Work Experience

Company _____

Address _____

Telephone _____

Job _____

Date: From _____   To _____

Work Experience

Company _____

Address _____

Telephone _____

Job _____

Date: From _____   To _____

Signature _____

Match.

1. Do you have a job? — — — — — — — — — — — —   Eight hours a day.

2. What do you do?   I'm a sales clerk.

3. How many hours do you work?   Yes, I do.

4. Do you work Monday to Friday?   12:30 p.m.

5. What time do you go to work?   Yes, I do.

6. What time do you eat lunch?   8:00 a.m.

7. Do you have experience?   At ABC Factory.

8. Where?   Yes. I was a factory worker.

9. For how long?   Two years.

10. Please print your name.   Yes, he does.

11. May I help you?   John Lee.

12. Does he work 5 days a week?   I want to apply for a job.

Ask your classmates for their signatures.

A: Please sign your name.

B: OK. Where?

A: What's your last name?

B: _____

A: Sign here.

Last Names A to F	Last Names G to L
_____	_____
_____	_____
_____	_____
_____	_____

Last Names M to S	Last Names T to Z
_____	_____
_____	_____
_____	_____
_____	_____

Write one job in each box.

teacher	police officer	restaurant worker	security guard
bus driver	cafeteria worker	office worker	teacher's aide
sales clerk	mechanic	factory worker	garment worker
doctor	hospital worker	ambulance driver	dentist

Listen. Write an ✕ on the job that your teacher says. The students with all ✕s win.

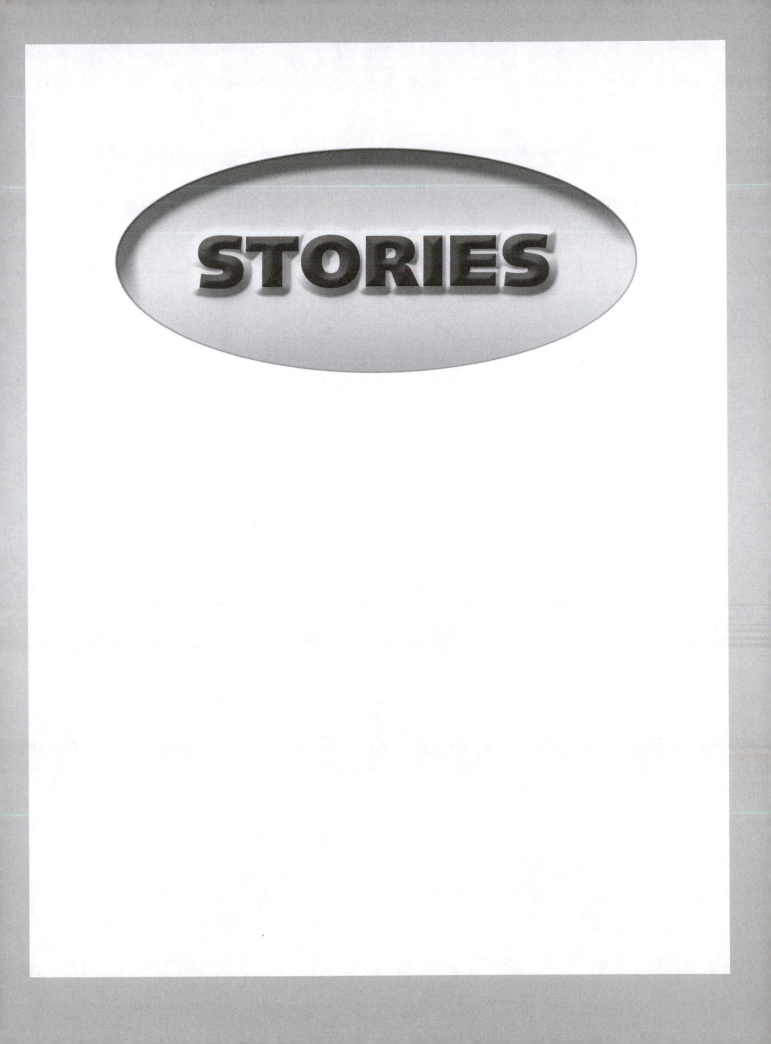

Read.

1.

I go to work.

2.

I go to school.

3.

I study English.

4.

I walk home.

Read.

1. I go to school.

2. I say hello to the teacher.

3. I sit at a desk.

4. I open my book.

5. I write in my book.

6. I write on the board.

Read.

1.

I get up at 7:00.

2.

I go to work at 8:00.

3.

I eat lunch at 12:00.

4.

I go to school at 6:30.

5.

I watch TV at 9:00.

6.

I go to sleep at 11:30.

UNIT 5 STORY

Read.

1.
I eat at a restaurant on Sunday.

2.
I go to the bank on Monday.

3.
I study English on Tuesday and Thursday.

4.
I go shopping on Wednesday.

5.
I clean the house on Friday.

6.
I do laundry on Saturday.

UNIT 6 STORY

Read.

I go to the market.

I get change.

I go to the bus stop.

I get on the bus.

I pay the exact change.

I take the bus to school.

Circle Yes **or** No **about the story.**

1.	I pay ten dollars.	Yes	(No)
2.	I go to the post office.	Yes	No
3.	I go to the bus stop.	Yes	No
4.	I get on the bus.	Yes	No
5.	I get a credit card.	Yes	No
6.	I take the bus to the bank.	Yes	No
7.	I take the bus to school.	Yes	No

UNIT 7 STORY

Read.

This is my sister.

She's from Mexico.

She's 25 years old.

She works every day.

She's a good student.

She's very busy.

Circle Yes **or** No **about the story.**

1.	My sister is from Mexico.	Yes	No
2.	She's 28 years old.	Yes	No
3.	She works every day.	Yes	No
4.	She's a good teacher.	Yes	No
5.	She's a good student.	Yes	No
6.	She's very worried.	Yes	No

Read.

I eat breakfast.

I drink coffee at work.

I eat lunch in the cafeteria.

I go shopping.

I cook dinner.

I have dinner with my family.

Circle Yes **or** No **about the story.**

1.	I eat breakfast.	Yes	No
2.	I drink milk at work.	Yes	No
3.	I drink coffee at work.	Yes	No
4.	I eat lunch at home.	Yes	No
5.	I go shopping.	Yes	No
6.	I cook dinner.	Yes	No
7.	I have dinner with my classmates.	Yes	No

UNIT 9 STORY

Read.

I feel well.

I exercise every day.

I eat fruits and vegetables.

I get checkups.

I don't smoke.

I sleep 7 hours.

Circle Yes **or** No **about the story.**

1.	I don't feel well.	Yes	No
2.	I exercise every day.	Yes	No
3.	I don't eat fruits and vegetables.	Yes	No
4.	I get checkups.	Yes	No
5.	I smoke.	Yes	No
6.	I don't smoke.	Yes	No
7.	I sleep 5 hours.	Yes	No

UNIT 10 STORY

Read.

This is John Lee.

He's a factory worker.

He works at TG Auto.

He works 8 hours a day.

He works 5 days a week.

He doesn't work Saturday and Sunday.

Circle Yes **or** No **about the story.**

1.	This is John Lopez.	Yes	No
2.	He's a restaurant worker.	Yes	No
3.	He's a factory worker.	Yes	No
4.	John works at TG Auto.	Yes	No
5.	He works 5 hours a day.	Yes	No
6.	He works 5 days a week.	Yes	No
7.	He works Saturday and Sunday.	Yes	No